HOPE MARKERS

How Hope Marks Your Story and Changes the World

JOAN GALLAGHER

©2016 Joan Gallagher. All rights reserved.
Hope Markers written by: Joan Gallagher.

www.relevantpagespress.com
www.joangallaghernowo.com

Published by Relevant Pages Press, Charleston, South Carolina No part of this book may be used or reproduced by any means, graphic, electronic, or mechanical, including photography, recording, taping or by any information storage retrieval system without the written permission of the publisher except in the case of brief quotations embodied in critical articles and reviews.

Scripture quotations are taken from the following biblical translations:

Scriptures taken from the Holy Bible, New International Version®, NIV®. Copyright © 1973, 1978, 1984, 2011 by Biblica, Inc.™ Used by permission of Zondervan. All rights reserved worldwide. www.zondervan.com The "NIV" and "New International Version" are trademarks registered in the United States Patent and Trademark Office by Biblica, Inc.™

Scripture taken from The Voice™. Copyright © 2008 by Ecclesia Bible Society. Used by permission. All rights reserved.

Scripture quotations are taken from the Holy Bible, New Living Translation, copyright ©1996, 2004, 2007, 2013, 2015 by Tyndale House Foundation. Used by permission of Tyndale House Publishers, Inc., Carol Stream, Illinois 60188. All rights reserved.

Scripture quotations from THE MESSAGE. Copyright © by Eugene H. Peterson 1993, 1994, 1995, 1996, 2000, 2001, 2002. Used by permission of NavPress. All rights reserved. Represented by Tyndale House Publishers, Inc.

Cover design by Zach McGinnis.
Interior Layout by Betts Keating Design.

ISBN: 978-0-9982211-5-1
Printed in the United States of America.

Table of Contents

This book is dedicated to all the brave women I know who have looked to the hope revealed in their stories and walk the path with the One who saves – Jesus Christ.

Acknowledgments

My heart's desire for this book is that people will be pointed to Jesus Christ for their journey. I pray I've been obedient with every word written. The journey with Him is the greatest adventure we can ever travel. I love you Abba.

To the love of my life, Ed. You champion me, love me, and inspire me. This project started at your urging because you have always believed in me and in God's calling on my life. No words come close to how thankful and blessed I am living this life with you.

Thank you Adam and Zach. Your expertise and encouraging feedback all along the way have made this project so much more meaningful for me. Meg, you humbly offered your story for this book, it is a powerful love-message. You are a World-Changer. Andy, one day you said to me, "Mom, I'm really proud of you for doing this." Your words have held me up and it meant more to me than you'll know. I am taken aback that God loves me so much he would give me all of you as my sons, daughter, and son-in-law. I love you all.

To the most incredible group of women a girl can have helping on a project: Stephanie, Jennifer, Betts, Steph, Elizabeth, Lara, Joanie, Sharon, Laura, Jennifer, and Jean. You all read, edited, gave great feedback, talked me down off ledges, prayed for me, and loved me so well.

To the many who have encouraged me and prayed for me: Thank you! I'm not sure I could even begin to name you all or find a way to express my heart of gratitude for you. Please know you are loved and prayed for with misty eyes quite often.

Introduction

A little-known story offers a compelling perspective on the adventurous journey we can have in our life of faith.[1] When a great fire swept through the city of London in the 1600's it razed buildings, took life, and left ashen remains of the hopes and dreams of the people who lived there. One of the buildings destroyed was St. Paul's Cathedral, a beacon that pointed people to God. Architect Christopher Wren took on the task of building a structure that had the potential to rebirth hope from the ashes. One day he walked through the worksite as he oversaw the reconstruction. He came across one of the workers laying bricks and asked him what he was doing.

"What does it look like? I'm laying bricks," the worker replied.

---

[1] The Minor Prophets: God Still Speaks; Tom Cowan, with Kyle White; Christianity Today, November 8, 2015, chapter 11, p. 64.

Christopher continued to walk the site and discovered a second bricklayer. He asked the second worker what he was doing.

The second bricklayer responded, "I'm earning a living."

Later, Christopher approached a third bricklayer and asked him the same question he had asked the other two workers.

The third worker, with a glimmer in his eyes, exclaimed with passion, "I'm building a great cathedral for Almighty God!"

Each of these bricklayers started out at the same place in their "cathedral-building" journey: laying bricks. Yet their perspectives of their journeys clearly varied in purpose and inspiration. Their outlooks not only marked their futures, but also the futures of others. Each brick served as a marker of progress on the journey to build a grand future cathedral. Each marker placed brought the reality of hope and promise closer and closer to the people.

The first bricklayer could not see past the monotony of laying one brick after another. For him, the past grandeur of the original cathedral provided little to no inspiration. His lack of vision for the completion of the magnificent project impacted his perspective of the future. He just laid brick after brick after brick. He didn't choose to see markers of hope. He just saw piles of clay.

The second bricklayer could see past his tedious actions to realize the fruits of his labor. He understood that this job at least provided for his needs. He too did not gain inspiration from the past grandeur of the original cathedral as a motivation to live a more awakened present and vibrant future. He was unable to see his work as part of a beautiful future creation of markers that could help point others to God.

The third bricklayer was more than just a bricklayer; he was a master craftsman who understood how the past, present and future were interwoven with each brick he laid. He knew the original cathedral served as a marker of hope for all who visited it time after time. The cathedral marked a place where hundreds of people had met God. The third bricklayer understood his actions impacted the future for generations of people who would be inspired by the new cathedral. He knew each brick he laid would serve as a tiny marker of potential future impact on the generations of people who would come to the new cathedral.

Like the third bricklayer, this book is intended to help you understand how identifying the markers of your past can help you to better understand your present and then impact the trajectory of your future. Our stories are filled with people and events that influence who we become while traveling the path God has put before us. Therefore, our journey begins with knowing our own story. Then we can identify the important Hope-Markers. Ultimately, we will come to a place of holding up those Hope-Markers triumphantly and then going on to using our influence to help change the world, one story at a time. As you see God's intricate involvement in your story and your Hope-Markers take shape, I pray it will spur on a life lived more audaciously for Him and inspire relationships that change the world.

PART ONE
Preparing for the Journey

CHAPTER ONE
Your Story Matters

The Ladies of She Speaks

My car moved steadily through the winding roads of the West Virginia mountains on my way to the She Speaks Conference in Charlotte, North Carolina – the She Speaks Conference is an event created by Proverbs 31 Ministries to equip women in their calling to leadership, writing and speaking. I was excited, nervous and in awe. I still couldn't believe I would be among the throngs of over 800 women who would be attending this sold-out conference. Like me, some would be first-time attendees beginning a new adventure with God, while others would be more experienced with published books and full speaking schedules. It didn't matter how far one was on their journey though. At She Speaks, women come together to learn and encourage one another on their journey.

In the months leading up to the conference, women began

to get acquainted on social media through the She Speaks Facebook page and found commonality, close proximity, and kindred heart stories. Some formed groups based on common areas of focus and chose to meet separately at the onset of the conference. I desired this type of connection as well, but even for an extrovert like me, going into this unfamiliar world seemed a little daunting. Somehow, in God's quiet and powerful movements, He led me to an eclectic assortment of women who would also be attending the conference. We came from all different parts of the country – the charming South, the beautiful beachfront, the hearty Midwest and the sprawling expanse of Texas. While initially our stories seemed impossibly different, we found commonality in our desire for the love of God and what He'd called us to do.

We decided to meet for dinner the night before the start of the conference to get to know one another. I got there a little early to make arrangements so we would have enough room for our group. Of the eight other women, I only personally knew one of them beforehand, my friend, Elizabeth. Even though I knew no one else, it was evident when a woman who was part of our group walked into the restaurant. Each one had a hopeful look on her face as she scanned the restaurant for us, and an eagerness emanating from her spirit in anticipation of the adventure we were about to take together.

When all nine of us were finally seated around the table, I felt overwhelmed with the goodness of God and how he had brought this group of women together. We varied greatly in ages; some of us were professionals, others full-time moms, and still others were empty-nesters. But, we all found a connection when we shared our stories.

Over the course of the evening, one by one, each woman

poured out her heart in a way that would have made anyone listening think we were longtime friends. Some struggled through the pain of divorce while others shared stories of grounded marriages. Several women struggled with illnesses that relentlessly came up against them. There were those who counted the cost of brutal pasts but who knew healing with Jesus. Through the sharing of our stories that night it became clear God was using our pasts to point people to His message of hope.

Because We Matter to God

What I took away from that evening is this: the story of our life matters. It matters, first and foremost, because we matter to God. He loves us and desires to heal our hurts and show us how the struggles we encounter can be used to move us closer to God, so we can live the rich life He has for us. No matter what pain fills our stories, when we invite God in, we can receive healing. That act of healing empowers our present and impacts the future in ways we cannot fathom. I saw the healing and empowerment that can only come from God play out that evening. As I witnessed these women share their stories, I saw how much everyone else at the table was empowered and inspired by them as well. This is the beauty of an embraced story. Even our most pain-filled times, with God's healing, can go on to inspire and point others to the incredible power of our God.

I'm a poster child for this truth. Growing up my behavior was characterized by performance-based living and much of my self-worth came from athletics. If we won, I felt I would be accepted and receive approval. If we lost, worthlessness reigned in my heart as the criticism snarled and took chunks of life out of me. This same perception of my worth permeated in other areas of my life as well, until I felt lost in a sea of trying to gain approval through what I did, never believing who I was could ever be enough.

After inviting God into my story, I began to see finding my worth in the fickle opinions of others was not His way for me. He had created a new standard in my life. I no longer needed to jump wherever approval awaited; I knew I was "approved of" no matter what. I no longer needed to please others for my own worth. Instead, my focus became a desire to honor God with what He had given me. God patiently continues to work in this area of my life. I am a work in progress, but God is my source for healing and direction every time this old way of thinking tries to invade my mind.

I shared with my She Speaks friends about how I was learning to overcome the need to live a performance-based life. At the table with those women that night, I chose to tell the story of how God has redeemed me from seeking the approval of others. To my surprise, God then used my story to touch one of those women. All her life she had struggled with the lie that the approval of others determines her self-worth. Seeing how God had shown me this truth and what He had done in my life through it, gave her encouragement to seek His truth for herself. I was able to share my story and, because of His mercy, soon this woman will do the same for someone else.

Whatever is in your past, whatever tragedy holds you, God wants you to know a present and future filled with healing and hope. Just like my friend and me, God wants to show you His view of who you are and what he has for you: healing and hope. Once healing begins, our actions start to change as well. In Romans it tells us:

> *Do not conform to the pattern of this world, but be transformed by the renewing of your mind. Then you will be able to test and approve what God's will is - His good, pleasing and perfect will.* Romans 12:2, NIV

We are transformed by the renewing of our minds when we allow God's truth into the perspective we have of the past. As He frees us from our worldly thinking of our pasts, we come to understand the truth about how much He loves us, the freedom that is ours, and His will for our daily lives.

God wants to bring change into your life based on the reconciliation of your past with His view of you. Remember, you are His beloved and are a part of his grand tapestry. He wants you to live and embrace a victorious life instead of a defeated life based on the pain of your past and the values of this world. A transformed life comes from allowing God to do His work of healing your past. That healing starts in your

Remember, you are His beloved and are a part of his grand tapestry. He wants you to live and embrace a victorious life instead of a defeated life based on the pain of your past and the values of this world.

present as you begin the journey to accept His truth about who you are and what He has for you.

Eyes to See

The process of healing within our story also produces for us an awareness of others' pain. We are given the ability to see others' struggles as it relates to the struggles of our pasts. Then we can have the grace to share our healed pasts as a way to encourage others to invite God into their pain as well. While our healing was meant just for us, God gives us opportunities to join Him in weaving it as a part of His tapestry of love for all of us.

That night at the restaurant, God revealed to all of us how He had woven together our life's hurts into a reflection of how much He loves us. We began to experience "Me Too!" moment after "Me Too!" moment as we not only revealed the pain of our pasts but also shared the redemptive healing of God's grace. When one of my new friends shared her heartache over her divorce, another spoke up, "Me too! I've been where you are." The one just beginning this difficult road of loss and healing found she had an experienced, kindred journey-woman who could encourage her on a path she herself was just starting. I felt my own common bond when I shared my struggle with being an empty-nester with another woman who found herself just beginning this same journey. These "Me too!" moments are how God uses our past to touch the lives of others as we choose to trust Him and courageously venture out to share our life experiences.

In scripture, we have an example of the redemption of a past that impacted a present and empowered others' futures.

You're probably familiar with Paul, but have you ever seen him as a compelling story-teller?

Paul's Story

Paul was a storyteller. He often told and re-told the stories of how God had worked in his life and ministry. He was born a Jew and citizen of Taurus. He was trained as a Pharisee like his father. He became so zealous in his persecution of Christians that he hunted them down and had them killed. Then Jesus stepped in. Jesus appeared to Paul on the road to Damascus and declared himself to be Jesus of Nazareth, the Lord of the very people Paul was persecuting. Paul went to Damascus where he met a man named Ananias. Ananias told Paul to ask for forgiveness and be baptized. That is when Paul was transformed and began his life of following Christ (see Acts 22-28 for more on Paul's story).

Paul spent the rest of his life telling as many as he could about his story. He shared how God had rescued him from a life of darkness. God also healed Paul from a past of prideful worldly knowledge and bitterness and hate of those who knew the true knowledge of God. Paul embraced his past in the light of God's transforming power and then used his story to point others to Jesus Christ.

> *At once, he began to preach in the synagogues that Jesus is the Son of God. All those who heard him were astonished and asked, 'Isn't he the man who raised havoc in Jerusalem among those who called on this name? And hasn't he [Jesus Christ] come here to take them as prisoners to the chief priests?' Yet Saul [Paul] grew more and more*

powerful and baffled the Jews living in Damascus by proving that Jesus is the Christ. Acts 9:20-22, NIV

Paul's story can be used as an example for us, giving us hope and strengthening our belief that the stories of our past can be redeemed. His past overflowed with bitterness, rage, hatred, and pride, yet Jesus loved him and came to give him healing. Paul's salvation changed everything and brought healing to his present; no longer tied to his past, his present changed drastically from one of a murderer in the name of God to "an apostle of Christ Jesus by the will of God" (Ephesians 1:1, NIV). Even though it took a while for the people he had hurt to trust him, he was given the strength and wisdom to share his story and offer hope to others. He was inspired by hope to continue trusting in God for his future, in spite of his past. We have access to this hope as well for the redemption of our past, the healing of our present, and a fulfilling, healthy future.

God gave one of the women I met at She Speaks opportunities to share her story after a year and a half of living with a chronic disease. For months, she was dependent on her family for all of her needs. Once a woman who was needed by many, she was now a woman who could do nothing without other's help. At one desperate point, she chose to allow God to move in and help her leave behind the "I-can-do-it-all" woman she had been. The result was a renewing of her mind that transformed her into a "dependent-on-God" woman. Her past experiences of hurt that led to her choosing to rely only upon herself were redeemed so that her present was healed from those behaviors that kept her locked into her own self-sufficiency. These experiences, from God's perspective, now

> *Your story matters. You matter enough to God that He not only desires to redeem your story, but to give you the privilege to be a part of how He redeems others stories.*

defined her purpose and influenced how she lives in her present. She had resolved to walk alongside others with a similar story.

Your story is as powerful as my friends'. Both triumph and tragedy mark your story as well. In God's perspective both are essential to His plan for your life. As you invite Him into your story and receive His healing of your present, He will guide you to share your story and find moments of commonality with others in "Me too!" moments, offering another reason to hope. This storytelling and commonality is a picture of how God wants us to live in the future. We are all encouraged to build each other up; in essence to become journey-women that are committed to the journey God calls us to travel.

Your story matters. You matter enough to God that He not only desires to redeem your story, but to give you the privilege to be a part of how He redeems others' stories. But how does He do this? How can you recognize when God is moving inside your story? He uses things I like to call Hope-Markers.

CHAPTER TWO
The Woman Not So Unlike Us

Scripture tells us about a woman who had continuous bleeding for twelve years (Mark 5:25). All of her resources were depleted and any hope she'd had of healing was long gone. One day, she heard Jesus was coming to her town. I imagine that day probably looked something like this:

> *She mustered whatever small semblance of strength she had after a painful, frustrating night of sleeplessness. She felt weak and anemic, and no amount of rest would help her feel better. She didn't dare to dream of healing anymore. Every bit of money she had was gone, spent on doctors who could not help her. To add to her pain, it had been a long time since she'd been nourished by a healthy meal. But even a lack of food did not hurt as*

much as hearing the cries of "Unclean! Unclean!" anytime someone saw her. This label followed her everywhere. According to the law, anyone or anything that touched her would also be considered unclean Leviticus 15:19-30. *Everyone stayed away. She was an outcast and loneliness gripped her* Mark: 5: 25-27, Luke 8:43-48, Matthew 9:20-2.

Let's pause in the story to reflect. Our stories aren't too far off from this woman's when you think about it. We may not have people yelling, "Unclean! Unclean!" as we walk down the street, but they may think something mean or unfair as we go by. They may turn to whisper to a friend, "Did you hear about her? She used to…" (We can all fill in a different phrase in to finish that sentence, can't we?). The whispers might be about poor choices we've made in the past, questions about how we're living in our present, or a simple disregard for the possibility of a celebrated future. All those shouting, "Unclean! Unclean!", whether to the woman in the first century or in modern terms to us today, have greatly underestimated the power of the hope we have in Jesus Christ.

Finding Hope

Hope can be defined as a person or thing in which expectations are centered.[2] The woman hoped against all the odds that Jesus was the person she could rest all her expectations of healing. He had already revealed himself to many as the

---

[2] Definition of "hope" as "a person or thing in which expectations are centered." www.dictionary.com/browse/hope?

answer for all who hoped for a better present and future. So, how did hope change this woman's life 2,000 years ago? Let's pick the story back up:

> *It was time for her to approach Jesus to ask for her impossible healing. She'd managed to make it to the road where she saw a crowd forming. There were people everywhere. Young and old, women and men, people of means as well as those with nothing were there, but everyone stayed away from her. After all, who wanted to take the risk of touching her and becoming unclean just as Jesus came down the street?*
>
> *She heard murmurings that Jesus would be passing her way very soon. The woman worried about her insignificance in Jesus' eyes. Her courage began to falter. Why would he have any concern for her and her endless unclean state?*
>
> *Hope started as a tiny bud as she saw a large group coming down the street. If she could move up close enough to just touch the hem of his garment, she knew healing would come. But what if he was angry she touched him? Could he become defiled by her touch?*
>
> *There wasn't much time to debate with herself. When she saw the strong, tall Centurion coming down the street, she knew Jesus was near. She gathered up as much strength as she could as she made her way to the side of the road. She waited for her chance to squeeze through the massive crowd. Finally, a break seemed to come for her. Jesus would walk right near her and he was on her side of the crowd.*

> *Her moment had arrived! She saw the fringe of his cloak, and she pushed through the crowd. She did not care if she touched someone; it was worth the risk if it meant healing. She told herself: If I just touch his clothes, I will be healed.* Mark 5:28, The Voice

So what happened next? The best part of the story came after her step of faith. She managed to just get the hem of Jesus' cloak in her fingertips when immediately her bleeding stopped. Jesus, after calling out to whomever had touched him, turned to her and said, "My daughter, your faith has saved you; go in peace and be whole from your disease" (Mark 5:34, The Voice).

Can you imagine? He healed her! She had been right to have hope.

The woman had exhausted all hope for healing yet her decision to step out and dare to hope again that Jesus would heal her was a major event in her life; one that would change her life both in the present and the future. She found hope in the opportunity for healing as well as in the person of Jesus Christ. This event and the person of Jesus became what I like to call "Hope-Markers" in her life.

Markers of Hope

We all have stories filled with important markers of hope. Hope-Markers point us to the path God is calling us to travel. It can be a person, an event (positive or negative), and even our everyday happenings. A deeper look into Hope-Markers shows how God can plant them in our lives to lead us where He wants us to go.

God also allows us to plant Hope-Markers in our lives that represent certain events we learned from or people who have had an influence in our life. We firmly plant these Hope-Markers on our path to remind us of all that God has done to encourage us for our future, and as a source for those coming up behind us on their own journeys. Influential people who are Hope-Markers in our pasts, both positive and negative, point us to the type of people and relationships we want for the future and even all God is calling us towards in our story.

Let me give you an example from my own life. My college roommate, Angela, was a godly example and a powerful influencer in my life. She was, and is, a Hope-Marker I planted because she taught me to stay anchored to God and His truth. She introduced me to a loving God who delights in me, and who desires a one-on-one relationship with me. The idea that God wanted to have this kind of bond with me had never occurred to me, nor had it been expressed to me. It was a revolutionary truth in my life; one that marked my story with hope in the midst of a painful past and so she and her influence in my life have become a Hope-Marker of all God has redeemed in my life.

Negative people can also be used as Hope-Markers. They show us what we don't want to become or what we should not accept in life as influence. They point us away from harm so we can stay on the path towards a life with God. Several damaging relationships from my past left me empty with feelings of worthlessness. I didn't believe I deserved more than the meager scraps of attention I sporadically received from these people. Buried deep in my heart, however, was a desire for more. A small bud of hope, barely alive, yearned to feel special and prized. These hurtful people serve as markers of hope because they remind me that I don't ever want to live with such damaging relationships in my life. I now know these people are God's Hope-Markers for me, reminding me that He desires for me to have loving, encouraging and inspiring relationships.

Tragedies, struggles, and celebrations mark our path in definitive ways unique to each of us. Our stories are not only distinguished by success or living a good life. Adversity and affliction also leave impressions on our lives, but they too ultimately point us to the King who always wins.

Not all Hope-Markers Are Happy

The truth of this type of Hope-Marker came unexpectedly in my life as a teenager. One cold December morning, at the age of 15, I sat in my room frozen by the sound of my mother's gut-wrenching cries. I knew something was desperately wrong, but the unknown truth kept me firmly planted on the edge of my bed. I knew I should be getting ready for school, but

Our stories are not only distinguished by success or living a good life. Adversity and affliction also leave impressions on our lives, but they too ultimately point us to the King who always wins.

instinctively I knew that school was not going to be a part of my day. Neighbors started to come to our house. My other siblings began to wake, and I was slowly enveloped by the realization that someone had died. But who?

My father was out of town. Could it be him? No, I heard my mom tell some unknown voice she had reached him, and he was on his way home. I eventually learned it was my brother, Nick. He was only 21 years old. He, along with another brother of mine, Dan, were out the previous night and had slammed a car into a telephone pole. Nick was gone. I would never see his handsome smile light up a room or hear him call me by my nickname, "Bones."

I somehow navigated the remainder of my freshman year of high school. His death left me asking questions I wrestled with for years to come. After all, what does a 15-year-old know about death and what to do with it? One thing I quickly learned was that our family would never be the same again. We were to carry on with little spoken of it. The pain and discomfort of loss pressed down hard and kept me from speaking about it, and I heard no one else express their grief.

Nick's death and my struggle to understand it left a large Hope-Marker in my life. It's my constant reminder that God is in control of all things, even death and life. After Nick died, I was fearful of death. I thought a lot about when and how it would happen for me. His death brought me to a pivotal place of struggle with God and whether he truly had a plan for my life or if it would come to a pointless end.

I found myself asking God many questions because of this major event in my life. As I grew older and asked these questions, there were people who pointed me to a loving God who indeed has a plan for my life. It sent me to my knees, praying to accept Jesus as my Savior in part because He knows what it feels like to live this finite life with the hope of eternity spent with the Father. He knows because He himself experienced it:

> *When I saw him, I fell at His feet as though dead. Then He placed His right hand on me and said: 'Do not be afraid. I am the First and the Last. I am the Living One; I was dead and behold I am alive forever and ever! And I hold the keys of death and Hades.'*
> Revelation 1: 17-18, NIV

Sometimes Hope-Markers are created by the circumstances of our lives or other's lives. I had no control over the death of my brother, but I chose to solemnly plant it as a Hope-Marker in my life. It reminds me to trust the true God who has power over all things and desires to be by our side in the struggles of life.

When we choose to mark our stories, we transform our lives. No longer does our story define us with such labels as "unclean," "inconsequential," "useless," or whatever other labels are shoved at us by the enemy. Instead, our stories are used as markers to guide the trajectory that God is calling us to follow.

When we choose to mark our stories, we transform our lives.

Before There Was GPS

As a little girl, I remember looking at a map when we traveled. There were no handheld devices or a computerized voice telling us when to turn. I would watch the markings on the map as we drove along and felt excited when the mile-markers matched what I thought would come next based on the map. One of the things that I felt quite intrigued with were the mile-markers we passed. When on a familiar journey, like going to Grandma's, I knew what restaurants and gas stations we would pass at certain mile-markers. Pride swelled when the city I predicted would be the next one that whizzed by us with a sign announcing, "Welcome to..."

These mile-markers gave comfort and assurance that we were traveling the right way. They allowed context for how much of the journey we had left and how far we had gone. I liked how the mile-markers coincided with what the map said would be coming next. It made me feel secure. Occasionally, when we would be traveling in unfamiliar territory, Dad would pull over and get out the map to see just where we needed to go to get back on track again to reach our destination. A map clearly shows us what direction to take, with distinct mile-markers to aid in our choices and direction for our future.

Just as mile-markers lead us on the path to our destination, so too do Hope-Markers guide us on our journey through life. Considering the stories of our lives emphasizes these key markers. Hope-Markers help to bring clarity as we map out our present with God to bring honor to Him and purpose for us.

We can look for Hope-Markers in our story by asking ourselves a few key questions:

When we pay attention to how Hope-Markers influence our lives and why they are important, we partner with Jesus to not only mark our path but also to help others on their journey.

- When did we put our full hope in God to walk our journey with us?
- What event/s led us to a deeper trust in His will for us?
- Who did God place in our life to stretch us, or lead us, or rescue us?

When we pay attention to how Hope-Markers influence our lives and why they are important, we partner with Jesus to not only mark our path but also to help others on their journey. When we learn to use Hope-Markers in our lives, the outcome of this connectedness with Jesus Christ is a present filled with peace, a future poised to flourish, and an opportunity to point others to the same connection with the great God of love.

CHAPTER THREE
How Hope Marks Your Story

In chapter two, the woman with the bleeding issue was at a pivotal point in her story. The events in her past left her to believe healing would never come. Then news came that Jesus was in town. She dared to believe that Jesus could be the answer for her healing if she could just touch His cloak. That moment became a Hope-Marker in her life and revealed what she placed her hope in: Jesus Christ.

As her fingers grazed his cloak, health and energy surged through her body. He had made her whole again! But her happiness was short-lived. Jesus stopped in his tracks and looked around at the crowd pressing in on Him. The woman feared Jesus would be angry that she dared touch Him. The book of Mark describes the scene:

At once Jesus realized that power had gone out from him. He turned around in the crowd and asked, 'Who touched my clothes?'

You see the people crowding against you,' his disciples answered, 'and yet you can ask, Who touched me?'

"But Jesus kept looking around to see who had done it, then the woman, knowing what had happened to her, came and fell at his feet and, trembling with fear, told him the whole truth. He said to her, 'Daughter, your faith has healed you. Go in peace and be freed from your suffering.'
Mark 5:30-34, The Voice

The story ends there. We never read any more about the woman. We don't even know her name, but she is far from being unimportant. Hope stirred her heart to step out. She dared to believe healing was possible for her. Jesus didn't stop to ask her what she had done to bring about her suffering. He didn't attempt to assess her sins or assign blame. Instead, He commended her for her faith and claimed healing over her life. It was countercultural.

Where Hope and Jesus Intersect

Here we see an illustration of the spiritual connection between Hope and its source – Jesus Christ. The moment of healing was a Hope-Marker for her. It was a stake in the ground that she could use to redirect the trajectory of her life from that point forward. Jesus offers these gifts to us today as the source of our hope: the opportunity to use Hope-Markers in our own story. The chance to change the trajectory of our lives.

One of the Hope-Markers that marked my story came at a trying time for my husband, Ed, and me. Our children were young and money was tight. We decided to take a risky step and went into business with friends. We wrongly put hope in our abilities rather than in God's plan. We thought we had mutual goals with our friends: a successful business in which we would conservatively put money away for the future. However, it was clear early on they instead wanted to benefit financially right away and liberally took money from the company.

Panic set in when we found out there were loans and debts we knew nothing about but were responsible for as part owners of the company. We had foolishly looked the other way when our partners spent money wherever and however they liked, and now it was all crashing in on us. When we started asking questions, they wanted us out. Several months later we decided we no longer wanted to be a part of the business, but there was a big problem. We needed our partners to sign a document relieving us from all the debt for us to be freed from the company. This was an impossible idea in our minds because they blamed us for the state of the company's tenuous financial situation. We felt stuck in a place we thought we would never get out of: hopelessly in debt and bound to the business partners who were keeping us hostage with lies. Our stress levels were running high, and we needed relief.

One night, as Ed and I sat quietly talking, we realized we needed to go to God and ask for His help; there was no other way out. We prayed for forgiveness for stepping out without coming to Him in the first place and asked for Him to show us what to do. We made a conscious effort to put our hope in God, pray, and wait for Him to lead our steps. A faithful friend called one day soon after and told us of an attorney who could help us. Our first response was discouragement; our narrowly focused eyes only saw how expensive it could be to hire an attorney and not that God was making a way for us. Our friend urged us to call and at least talk with him since the first consultation was free.

A few days later we walked into the lawyer's office. His kind, soft spoken demeanor put us at ease as we settled into the chairs across from him. He introduced himself and told us that our mutual friend had shared a little of our story. He said he wanted to do this work for us for free. We sat stunned. Immediately we knew God was in the midst and hope pulsated in our hearts.

We walked out of his office with a plan that had seemed impossible in our eyes: Get our name waived from all company debt, and the money we had invested in the company returned to us plus interest. Just like the woman who thought healing was impossible, so too did we think this solution would not come to pass.

Several weeks later our attorney met with our business partner and his lawyer to settle the dissolution of the partnership. Ed and I waited at home praying and keeping ourselves busy. The phone rang, and I instantly felt my stomach tighten as Ed answered the phone.

As he listened, Ed's tense face relaxed and broke into a joyful smile as he said, "How did you get him to agree to that?" After what seemed like a lifetime, Ed hung up the phone and just stared at me with the same joyful smile.

I asked urgently, "What did he say, what did he say?"

With a look of astonishment still on his face, he replied, "The lawyer got Mark to sign a document relieving us from all company debt and removing our name from the company. He also got him to agree to pay us everything we invested plus 10 percent interest."

"How did he get him to agree to that?" I asked in amazement.

"He told us not to worry about it; it was taken care of."

What started as a painful struggle that could have relegated us to a life of defeat, became a Hope-Marker to remind us of God's provision and His desire to lead us in every area of our life. As we learn to invite God's healing into the painful moments of our past, we can embrace the hope that is found and put our faith in its source.

> *Why am I overwrought? Why am I so disturbed? Why can't I just hope in God? Despite all my emotions, I will believe and praise the One who saves me and is my life.*
> Psalm 42:5, The Voice

The psalmist gives witness to the fact that there are moments in life where pain and worry overtake us. We can all remember moments in our past that caused us to feel such struggle. When we consider these moments through the lens of the hope God gives us, we can identify them as Hope-Markers. The woman with the bleeding issue, as well as Ed and I, moved from a place of feeling overwrought and disturbed because of the events in our lives to a place of hope in God. Our needs may not have been met right at the moment of understanding this truth, but when one hopes in God there is peace in waiting for His timing:

> *My soul quietly waits for the true God alone because I hope only in Him.* Psalm 62:5, The Voice

The beauty of Hope-Markers is that they don't outlive their usefulness. They become tools to remind us of how God has taken a difficulty in our life and used it to teach us, and others, about how to live more closely with Him. The results of embracing our stories and the Hope-Markers in them is a life lived confidently in the promises that God has for all His children. The Hope-Markers of our lives allow us always to have direction when we need guidance, confidence when there seems to be no solution, and peace no matter how difficult the struggle. How? Because they serve as reminders both of God's faithfulness no matter what we face in life and that God has made a way:

> *But those who trust in the Eternal One will regain their strength. The will soar on wings as eagles. They will run-never winded, never weary. They will walk-never tired, never faint.* Isaiah 40:31, The Voice

The struggles, pain, abuse, and heartbreak of your past matter. These experiences are valuable in the shaping of our presents and futures, even with the pain and trauma we have experienced. The woman who was bleeding couldn't see it at the moment, but her story, through the lens of God's perspective, mattered. Her trauma, her pain, and her abuse at the hands of those claiming her "Unclean!" were used by God to bring her to Jesus. Her choice to embrace Him brought her healing, which altered her present as she was able to enter into

Embracing our story is to acknowledge the painful moments of our past. Planting Hope-Markers is to look for where hope can be found, and allow our present to benefit from them.

the culture of the day. No longer the same woman, she began, simply by living and telling of what Jesus had done for her, to experience a change in the trajectory of her future, and affect change for others. She was saved by her faith which not only affected her, but effected change for all of us.

In the same way, my husband and I couldn't see that our struggle and pain mattered at that moment, but that experience has been valuable for us as well. It brought us closer to Jesus, our Redeemer, and altered our present by changing the financial path we chose to be on. Our future was significantly affected. We learned from this lesson and have chosen to seek God's direction before any major business decision (among other decisions as well). We have even seen how this experience has affected our children and other friends whom we have been led to share this part of our story.

Your story matters too. Inviting God into all the places of pain and struggle in your life to reveal His presence offers an opportunity for you to plant your own Hope-Markers. These markers will serve as guides to your healing and ultimately freedom from the after-effects of the pain and struggle you have experienced.

Embracing our story is to acknowledge the painful moments of our past. Planting Hope-Markers is to look for where hope can be found, and allow our present to benefit from them. But it's what we do with those Hope-Markers that can make all the difference in our futures.

PART TWO
Filling Your Backpack

CHAPTER FOUR
Pack Your Backpack

The summer before my second year of college was filled with trepidation. While I was fretting about the upcoming school year, the summer itself had also not panned out the way I had hoped. Instead of summer nights filled with fun and friends, both my days and nights were filled with strife. My parents and I struggled to connect, and I was at odds with my friends. I lashed out at those around me and then isolated myself from them. Unfortunately, because of this, the long-time friend I had planned on rooming with that following year decided she didn't want to be around me. I told her that was fine by me; I would take my chances with whoever would come my way. Yes, I was having an awful summer.

As the school year loomed closer, I began the usual preparations of packing the necessary belongings for college life. My favorite item was my trusty backpack. I could put enough in there to keep me alive for several days if needed. As

I packed it away in the tub of other items, I pictured myself with it slung over my shoulder as I ran from building to building to make a class, or having it with me when I went to the cafeteria to study and eat. Eating was another way I self-soothed when life was hard. It was easy to hide because I could participate in another activity of isolation: going for a long run. I planned on doing both of these things often since I seemed to struggle so much in my relationships.

Angela

God knew I would be without a roommate coming into that year and had already made plans for my life to intersect with someone special. Angela was different than anyone I had met before. She seemed genuinely happy to meet me. As we arranged our room, we got to know each other. Almost immediately she shared that she grew up in a Christ-centered home and that her parents daily modeled the love of God for her. That was something new for me and, to be honest, I wasn't quite sure what that all meant.

I could see how Angela treated others around her, though. She was beautiful and humble, and her passion was to model the love of Christ in the same way her parents did. She also desired to use the gifts and talents God gave her, so she worked diligently at her school work and she was a 4.0 student. Everything about her life exemplified a desire for this same excellence. She had a boyfriend who had the same passion for God that she had, and they had a desire for their relationship to honor God. During that year at college, I saw Angela was beautiful and humble and her passion to model the love of Christ was almost...palpable.

When we moved into our dorm room before school started, I made sure to set up a place for my backpack in its own special cubby spot next to my desk. I'd always liked having it close and would fill it with anything I thought necessary for my day. I felt comforted when I arranged books, snacks, pens, highlighters and whatever else I needed. I would rearrange it several times before I was satisfied with how it looked. As I look back, it was something in life I could control; carefully selected items arranged how I wanted. Angela, however, would show me a whole new way to pack a backpack. That year, she would become the Hope-Marker who would eventually teach me about the loving God who delights in His own.

My New Life

As the year went on, Angela patiently loved me and modeled God's tender ways to me each day. Watching her, a pang of hunger stirred within me to know Him more and to understand what my relationship with Him would look like. Eventually, she led me in a prayer of salvation.

It felt awkward at first. I didn't know how to start this new "saved" life. It was so opposite to everything I had known, and I was easily discouraged. When I talked to Angela about it, she encouraged me to pray and ask God to show me, through His Word, what he wanted for my life.

That didn't feel as easy as she made it sound. I wasn't comfortable talking to God. I wasn't even sure he listened to me. My prayers felt too plain and simple. And she said I would find answers in the Bible…How? I had never read the Bible before. It was so intimidating. Where would I even start?

Angela gently encouraged me: "He'll show you if you just ask."

One morning after she left for class, I scrambled to get my backpack packed for the day. I found myself wondering, as a new believer should I take the Bible with me? I wanted to, but its pages still seemed mysterious to me, and it felt strange to put it in my backpack. A Bible had certainly never been in there before. Somehow, a prompting invited me to sit at my desk with it before heading out to class. It felt awkward to even open it, but Angela's words would not leave me alone: "He'll show you if you just ask."

Ask? The question stuck in my mind. Why would God concern himself with one hurting girl sitting in her dorm room? He must certainly have too much on His plate! But I took a deep breath and quietly asked, "What comes next God?"

Fear set in. I felt I had made myself too vulnerable. Now I was stuck. What if God didn't hear me? Or worse yet, even cared to answer me? In the back of my mind, I knew I had my safety nets of control in the form of food and running I could fall back on, but they seemed like such empty solutions now. I very much wanted to hear from God.

I opened the Bible with shaky hands and my eyes immediately went to a few verses right on the opened page. My eyes focused right at a spot that seemed as if it was highlighted just for me:

> *'For I know well the plans I have in mind for you,' says the Lord, 'plans to prosper you and not to harm you, plans to give you hope and a future. When you call on me, when you go to pray to me, I will listen. When you seek me with*

all of your heart, you will find me with you and I will change your lot.' Jeremiah 29:11-14, NIV

I couldn't believe it. Did God have a plan for me? And a future filled with hope? As a new believer, this love-message from God seemed revolutionary. Another Hope-Marker was planted as I realized I wouldn't have to go through life trying to figure out what would please God because he had just given me the answer: 1) He has a plan filled with hope and an eternally prosperous future for me and 2) My part is to pray, listen, and seek Him.

This verse became a powerful tool in helping me discern other Hope-Markers He was laying out in my life. It urged me to forge ahead on my journey with God. But, I knew if I was going to be successful on this path He had placed me on, I needed to equip myself with tools to help me stay anchored to Him and follow His path. I realized I needed to pack my "spiritual backpack."

Packing your Spiritual Backpack

If you are packing a backpack for a hike, among the most important things you need to pack are the tools to guide you on your journey, a compass and a map. This same principle applies to packing our "spiritual backpack" as well. Scripture and prayer are a believer's map and compass. We need Scripture to chart our journey and prayer to keep us moving in the right direction. Why? Because we often find ourselves at a crossroads in life where we have a decision to make about what God would have us do in a given situation. God lays out the directions for the path He wants us to take through the

> *Scripture, brings hope, direction, correction and caution. It tells big, beautiful stories and gives sober warnings. It provides direction for our future and celebrates the greatness of God.*

map of His Word. Just as the map shows us the features of our surroundings so too does scripture show us the features of a life lived in Christ. We can then use prayer (our compass) to help point us in the right direction by going to our Heavenly Father and asking for guidance. Through scripture and prayer, God walks closely with us on our journeys as we make decisions for the way we should go.

Scripture: Our Spiritual Map

Scripture maps out how we are to live with God's direction. Scripture, brings hope, direction, correction and caution. It tells big, beautiful stories and gives sober warnings. It provides direction for our future and celebrates the greatness of God. There is always something new in the Bible to learn and be inspired by for our journey. Without seeking wisdom and truth from Scripture, we can end up in the thickets and weeds of a path far from God and filled with a world of doubt, confusion and sin. We must keep our map ever before us as we travel our journey, so this doesn't happen.

How we encounter God's Word in our daily lives is entirely up to us. We each were designed to have a relationship with

Him and to know Him and His Word helps us to do both. But, it is up to us to make sure we know God's Word. We can use Bible studies, topical studies, scripture sticky-notes on our dashboards and pop up reminders on our smartphones, among other things. There is no right way to keep scripture close to our hearts. Listed below are several suggestions to help you spend time in God's Word to impact your journey more powerfully. (Please know this isn't exhaustive. These are tips that have helped me over the years.)

1. Contemplate the Hope-Markers in your life that have had an impact on you. Then look to scripture to see what God's Word has to say about that particular topic. As an example, Angela was the Hope-Marker in my life that inspired me to want to know more about how to love others the way God loves because she modeled it for me. I went to the Bible to search for ways to do just that.

2. Be patient with yourself. Don't feel pressured that you have to read a certain amount in a certain period of time. Spend as much time as needed to understand what God is showing you in a passage, even if it means reflecting on one single word within that passage until you understand what God is saying to you.

3. Try going below the surface. A Bible commentary close by helps to look a little deeper at the context or meaning of a passage.

4. Consider the historical context of scripture. There are several questions to keep in mind as you delve into a

particular book: Who is the author? When was it written? What was the cultural, political, and spiritual climate of the time it was written? Who was the target audience of the writing? What are some of the key words and themes that you see throughout the book?

5. Understand what type of book within the Bible you are reading. Psalms and Proverbs, for example, are books of poetry. The gospels are historical accounts. The later chapters in the new testament such as Ephesians and Colossians are letters written to first-century Christians. It helps to know what kind of book you are studying because it puts them in perspective just like the difference in reading a history text or a book of beautiful poetry.

6. Look for points of emphasis in the passage. For example, if we read I Corinthians 13 we can tell that love is the focus because it is mentioned nine times in just 13 verses.

7. Look up additional verses. In the margin of many Bibles are scripture references to additional sections of scripture related to the ones you are reading. They help give further meaning, so take a minute to check them out and consider how the verses are connected.

8. Partner with another Christ-centered friend or mentor. Reach out to someone you trust and ask questions, especially if you really feel stuck on a particular verse or concept. Over the years I have gone to my pastor or a mentor to help me better understand.

9. Above all, pray. Ask God to reveal what He wants to teach you through the passage. How does the passage impact your daily walk with Him? Is He giving you a call to action? How does the passage draw you closer to Him in service, worship and your relationship with Him?

I have used these tips over the years to help me better understand my time with God in His Word. There are many additional Bible aids that we have close at hand in our information age. Seek out reliable resources that help you connect.

Prayer: Our Spiritual Compass

The next "tool" we must have in our backpack is prayer. Prayer directs us, just like a compass, and helps us use the Hope-Markers God places on our path more effectively.

Simply put, prayer is the time we spend with our heavenly Father. He wants us to get to know Him so He can show us that our story matters to Him. When I look back over my journey, my conversations with God served as my lifeline in the most trying circumstances as well as my point of praise and celebration.

What does prayer look like to you? Billy Graham said, "Prayer is simply a two-way conversation between you and God."[3]

---

[3] Billy Graham. Whatchristianswanttoknow.com. Retrieved on May 5, 2016 from whatchristianswanttoknow.com. Website: http://www.whatchristianswanttoknow.com billy-graham-quotes-22-great-sayings/

Jesus gave us a model for prayer in Matthew 6:5-13 (NIV):

Our Father in heaven,

hallowed be your name,

your kingdom come,

your will be done,

on earth as it is in heaven.

Give us today our daily bread.

And forgive us our debts,

as we also have forgiven our debtors.

And lead us not into temptation,

but deliver us from the evil one.

Otherwise known as the Lord's Prayer, these verses tell us to come to Him with humble, God-centered hearts. He then gives us a foundation for what our prayers should look like.

This passage can be a model for our own prayer life. Based on that, here are a few things to start with:

1. First, praise and thank our great and generous God.

2. Take your struggles and sins to Him. He calls us to a place of repentance.

3. Take your requests to Him. Nothing is too small or too big for God to handle.

Through our prayers He directs us, encourages us, and gently leads us to the next Hope-Marker He's placed in our path.

We can pray to God anywhere at any time, but remember to pray often. God loves us and wants to hear from us. I also encourage you to find a spot in your home where you can meet with God regularly. I have a particular chair I like to sit in and talk with Him. It feels conversational, and I can pour out my heart to Him. But I have to also admit at times I slide to the floor on my knees, either in repentance because once again I am in need of His forgiveness; or in praise and worship because I am in awe of my great God.

You may find you too have a comfortable chair, but you also may find you prefer a quiet spot outside, or that your best quiet place may be your car. Again, there isn't a right place to meet with God.

Additionally, we all have our own prayer language to communicate with God. This language is just the way we feel Him and hear His voice. It doesn't have to be a language in the literal sense of the word. Whether it is in music, nature, writing, reading or conversing with Him out loud, any means of communicating with Him will help you see He is leading you.

Deep, meaningful interactions with God through prayer help us to navigate our lives. Through our prayers He directs us, encourages us, and gently leads us to the next Hope-

> *When we use our Hope-Markers in conjunction with scripture and prayer, they lead us on a straight path with God.*

Marker He's placed in our path. Once our spiritual backpacks are equipped with the tools of scripture and prayer, we can confidently set out on the plans God has for us. Hope-Markers then become powerful guides on our journey as a way to map where God is leading us to in the present. The result: a powerful future infused with the plan of God.

Angela is a Hope-Marker on my life's journey to remind me of how the love of God is a powerful influence in others' lives. Because of her influence, I have been motivated to seek out scripture (my map) and use prayer (my compass) to learn how to love others in the way God calls me to love.

God has a desire to guide you in filling your own spiritual backpack with His map and compass for your life as well. He wants you to get to know Him by using these powerful tools so you can trust His direction when you come to a crossroads in your life. Whether you meditate on a single verse, work through an entire book, pray out in nature, or in a comfy chair, know His desire is to hold tightly on to your hand and lead you through whatever thickets and weeds you may be in, back onto His path for your life. When we use our Hope-Markers in conjunction with scripture and prayer, they lead us on a straight path with God.

CHAPTER FIVE
Seize Your Story

There was a time in Andrea's life when she allowed her story to hurt her more than help her. Feelings of guilt, shame, and worthlessness flooded who she thought she was and persuaded her actions. When I first met Andrea, she exuded confident expectation about life. As a greeter at church, she joyfully welcomed all who walked through the doors. One Sunday morning she asked if I had time to talk that week. When we met, it seemed to take a little more effort for her to bring forth her warm smile. She let her guard down enough with me to share that she felt stuck in a rut and did not know how to get free from it.

"So tell me a little more of your story, Andrea. Start wherever you would like," I encouraged.

"I grew up in a tight-knit family, but I've been pretty independent most of my adult life. I bought my first car at 18, supported myself and put myself through college," she started.

Andrea's description of her independence did not surprise me at all, not from the high-reaching, confident young woman sitting in front of me. Curiously she didn't share this information as a goal to check off her list. Instead, I heard in her voice a more confused tone, as if there was more behind the meaning of her statement.

She continued, "I don't know why but I have always felt that I had to prove myself worthy to someone else as if I have to earn it. Jesus is my Savior, but I don't feel worthy of Him. I know I've surrounded myself with people who do not have the same like-minded purpose as I do. I just don't know how to get back on track. I thought if you would mentor me it might help."

We agreed to meet regularly for prayer and study. During our time, she revealed she had been in a relationship that left her feeling worthless and fearful. She expressed anxiety at the thought of being alone the rest of her life and wasn't sure if she could find a healthy relationship. I encouraged her to seek out counseling to help her get a grasp on these feelings.

One day, Andrea revealed that a male friend of hers lived in her home. She convinced herself it was a good idea because he helped take care of the house and paid rent. He took advantage of her kindness, however, and she allowed it because she was afraid to be alone. Her self-worth became dependent on the approval of this man and the group of friends who were a part of their shallow community. She gave, they took. Those were the unspoken rules. She continued to desperately grasp for any morsel of affirmation they would give her. She tried to straddle two paths: This community's approval and walking the path of Jesus on her journey. Those paths were impossibly far apart, and she began to show the weary effects of this effort.

Over the next several months, Andrea chose to lay her backpack down and leave the path that Jesus had for her. She waded through the thick weeds of man's approval and continued to allow the pain of scars of condemnation from herself and others to pierce her soul. All her fears wrapped around her, and she felt frozen in place. Jesus the Rescuer never left Andrea, however, even in the depth of the weeds. One day, she just couldn't go on in this shallow lifestyle any longer. She called out to Jesus, and he lovingly carried her back to the right path. She picked up her backpack and placed it firmly on her shoulders. She got rid of the damaging relationships and chose to spend time with godly women who could help her navigate her journey with her map and compass. She no longer straddled both paths. The old hurtful way of shallow, false relationships was a distant one she would not revisit.

The fickle world we live in would no longer get to dictate her story. Andrea believed Jesus when He said He could help her. Bravely, Andrea seized her story and allowed Jesus to be the author once and for all. While Jesus planted Hope-Markers to guide her into the future of healthy relationship building, Andrea made a choice to follow them. Her Hope-Marker (the day she picked her backpack up again) is also a solemn reminder of what she never wants to return to. Andrea has used this Hope-Marker in others' lives to show them that God makes a way when we feel paralyzed amid the weeds and thickets.

> *Story seizing begins the very moment we invite God into the heart-wrestling of our stories so He can define the trajectory of our present and future.*

Seize Your Story

Seizing your story means you are firmly taking the reins of your life. You are no longer defined by the ugliness in your past, but instead, make the choice to let God become the Divine Definer of your future. Story seizing begins the very moment we invite God into the heart-wrestling of our stories so He can define the trajectory of our present and future. Heart-wrestling is painful. It means we have to acknowledge that our efforts to control our journey and make it meaningful fail in comparison with all God is waiting to do in us and through us.

Our maps and compasses are crucial to our story seizing. They allow us to take the time to stop and examine our story with a God-perspective. When we use prayer and scripture to honestly evaluate our lives, God is welcomed in to guide our way as we continue to travel our path. As we take the time to use our tools to navigate our stories, we can see Hope-Markers that God has placed in our lives. For instance, it was God's Hope-Marker planting of the meeting between Andrea and me that set into motion our mentoring relationship. She also planted Hope-Markers when she made a choice to end her unhealthy relationship with the male "friend" living in her home. This Hope-Marker helped her follow God's way and keeps her away from the thickets and weeds of man's approval.

Three guides can help you walk alongside God as you seize your story one moment at a time. When these guides are used under the compass of prayer and with the map of scripture we can walk a triumphant path with our Savior as He takes us to new places on the journey He has planned for us:

1. **Heart-wrestling:** Take time to consider your story in prayer, asking God to show you the moments that mark your story. These moments can become Hope-Markers. Spend time asking God to help you make an authentic evaluation of your past and current circumstances and how they can be used as Hope-Markers to guide you on your future path. Spend time in scripture. God reminds us throughout His word of the active part He plays in our life; it serves as a guide for the journey. Scripture maps out for us how we are to live more fully, be in relationships with others and walk more closely with Him.

2. **Journal your story:** Experiment with different styles of journaling that speak to how you are wired. You can use an audio recording and narrate, create a timeline, photo-journal, or write your story. Then take your story and compare it with what God says in his Word. Seek God in prayer for the direction He wants you to go within a particular area in your life.

3. **Pursue God-honoring relationships:** God's Word is filled with examples of believers looking to a brother or

sister in Christ to love them and point them to a closer relationship with God. Mentors can spend time with us in prayer and in God's word to help us refine our understanding of our stories with God's outlook. They also share their Hope-Markers that have been firmly planted along their journey.

Don't let these seemingly easy steps fool you. There are pitfalls in the path. We do live in a broken world, and we must be vigilant about where our focus lies. The enemy lurks behind the weeds and thickets. He tries to entice us with a false promise that living there is better. When those enticements come, and they will, we must keep our attention on the Rescuer, Jesus Christ, and what we know He believes about us: He loves us and knows we can't travel this journey without Him. Still, there are times we listen to the false promises, and we venture into the thickets and weeds. We get lost and injured, but the Rescuer is right there by our side, ever ready to guide us back to the good path He travels. The more we seek to seize our stories, the less frequently we will walk off our path, but it is a lifelong process and, all those pitfalls have the ability to become Hope-Markers both for ourselves and others.

Warning: Don't Lay Down Your Backpack

A particular Hope-Marker serves as a sober reminder of a time I laid my backpack down and wandered into thorny, painful thickets. When all three of my children were busily navigating through the unpredictable roads of adolescence, they participated in sports and were involved in church as well as other activities. Ed often traveled for work. I worked

> *When those enticements come, and they will, we must keep our attention on the Rescuer, Jesus Christ, and what we know He believes about us: He loves us and knows we can't travel this journey without Him.*

part-time at our church and coached high school basketball. As a family we were on the go all the time and the coordinating of schedules was a major project. Even with the busyness, my morning time with God in His Word and prayer kept me grounded and close to Him.

Then, I started to wander off course. I started missing time with God. It started as one or two days a week. I made the excuse that I could get so much more done before the kids got up in the morning if I shaved 10 minutes off the hour of my quiet time I spent with God. Then it became twenty minutes and eventually none at all. Didn't God see the relentless schedule on the calendar in my kitchen? Surely He would want me to get ahead of that busy day. At first, I thought it was a good idea; I could throw up a prayer to God as I walked out the door.

I had laid my tools aside. His Word and prayer were no longer my first thoughts or actions. I took the road that looked deceivingly easier. At first, I didn't give it a second thought. After all, things would slow down eventually. I was in church every Sunday and belonged to a weekly home-study group with other couples from church. Wouldn't that be enough?

I began to feel as if I was wandering. I didn't see Hope-Markers anymore, probably because I wasn't looking. I had left my tools behind, thinking I was familiar enough with them that I could pull out a scrap here and there to get me through the day. The result? I wandered into the familiar thickets of the world's approval and the weeds of attaining more. No longer was my path visible; I was too busy looking at what I wanted or what I thought benefited my family.

The only tools I used on this path were self-promotion and selfish motives. Instead of seeing my children, husband's, and my accomplishments as ways to humbly honor God and point the way to Him, I used them as opportunities to place our family on a pedestal for the world to see that we were special. But it wasn't enough to have the praises of others; I wanted more.

The world can never give us what God does. When we pursue the world's approval, it will always leave us searching for more. The tools of this world are useless and damage us more than help us. Why? Because they are always turned inward keeping us from God. They never lead outward towards Him. I used those worldly tools to attempt to promote one of my children over a friend's child. It did not honor God or love this family well. The result was the loss of a friendship and mourning for my sin that had separated me from God.

As I sat in the parking lot of school one day waiting to pick up my kids and rush them off to the next activity, I realized I had lost my way. I was on the wrong path with the wrong tools. The path did not progress forward but only led me deeper into the thickets and weeds. It was time to call out to the Rescuer and pick up my backpack again.

The beauty of the tools God provides is that they are always available right beside us and He is patiently waiting for us to pick them up. That afternoon I found myself clinging to them once again in tears and repentance. I just wanted God to lead me back to the path. This Hope-Marker planting moment serves as a reminder of what happens when I rely on the wrong tools of self-promotion and selfish motives. My tears and repentance helped me to pick up the tools of His Word and start the conversation with Him in prayer once again. They led me back to the path God called me to walk safely with Him. This Hope-Marker will always remind me of what I never want to be; a prideful person enslaved to this world.

It isn't a bad thing for a Hope-Marker to be a bit painful. I hold this prickly Hope-Marker close to my heart because it reminds me I never want to wander off the path of God and travel so deeply into such tangled thickets and choking weeds again. Holding these prickly Hope-Markers with care is important. They should never be allowed to pierce our heart with guilt and shame. They are simply a reminder of how God redeemed a part of our story.

You may have painful Hope-Markers too. Unpack these moments with God in prayer and through His Word. Entrust them to one you feel safe telling your story to. Remember that you are a daughter of the King and He desires redemption for your life. He is calling you back to His path for you, hand in hand with Him, using His tools that will never fail you. Your most difficult Hope-Markers will be powerful ways to remind you of how you don't want to live and that God's ways are trustworthy to lead you well on your journey.

Following the Path Alone

There are also moments when we don't always feel God's presence. We pray and read the Bible searching for the answer to our prayers. We may pray for a wayward child or a way out of an impossible situation at work. Sometimes our prayers beg for healing. Even if He seems distant, please know He is there. He hasn't gone anywhere. He promises that He will not leave or forsake His loved ones. Stay on the path and continue to use your two powerful tools, prayer and scripture:

> *The Lord is righteous in all his ways and loving toward all he has made. The Lord is near to all who call on him, to all who call on him in truth.* Psalm 145: 17-18, NIV

We know His Word is trustworthy, so keep reminding yourself that He and His Word will never fail you. If God is silent, He has a purpose that is for our benefit. He may be asking us to wait right at the place we are on our path. God is not calling us to an inactive period. On the contrary, He is calling us to pursue Him in prayer and in His word in patient expectancy for His plan to unfold. I find when I am in these moments that time spent in praise of His goodness and future plans fills me with peace while waiting.

God is the one who transforms our experiences, both the struggles, and triumphs, into Hope-Markers. He doesn't leave it as an impossible goal to achieve; He indulgently gives us all we need to have a relationship with Him. His tools are powerful implements that take our pasts, no matter what they look like, and turn them into a journey full of compelling Hope-Markers that help us live a life of a brave story seizer.

What is the result of our story seizing? A life turned over

We no longer allow our past to dictate who and what we are supposed to be and do. Instead, we have taken our story and put it through the filter of God's holy work of redemption.

to the work and will of God. When we acknowledge our stories, we take the healthy, hurting, and healed parts of our past and use them as Hope-Markers in not only our lives but in the lives of others as well. These Hope-Markers guide our passions and our lives so we become the reality of all God has for us. We no longer allow our past to dictate who and what we are supposed to be and do. Instead, we have taken our story and put it through the filter of God's holy work of redemption. He rescues our story and champions us to have victory over the hurting parts and rejoice over the healthy parts. We can rest, rejoice, and be rejuvenated knowing Jesus is right next to us as we walk our journey. We are more able to focus on His plan when we acknowledge our Hope-Markers and keep our tools close by our side to influence our journey.

PART THREE
Journeys Marked By Hope

CHAPTER SIX
The Overcomer: Meagan

When I first started writing this book my daughter Meagan's story continued to come to mind. It is rich with the tragic twists and turns that we often find on our journey in life as well as the rescuing message of the Savior. Meagan has chosen the path of life. She has embraced her story and seized it, planting Hope-Markers for her journey and is now using them to impact others. Her story is a practical example of how God is there no matter what we face, even when we choose to lay down our backpacks with the vital tools of our map and compass and find ourselves desperately lost in the weeds and thickets.

From the beginning, Meagan lived life as a grand opportunity for celebration. Growing up in Michigan, she loved everything about what life had to offer. Her two older brothers loved her and often gave her opportunities to join in their grand adventures. We also quickly saw her athletic ability; basketball and soccer came naturally to her. Early on she had a simple love for God and prayed with a fervency most would aspire to in their own walk.

Meagan's path into adolescence began to show cracks as she navigated through the busy life of school, athletics, and church events. From all outside appearances, she seemed to have the same carefree outlook on life as she did as a child. God and her family would always be the rock-steady haven she would turn to, but the desire for approval and acceptance pushed hard against her. The stress of a move to an unfamiliar state, the heartache of the first time she experienced scorn by a boy, the rejection of a friend she thought loved her, or the struggle to understand a math problem quickly disillusioned the once carefree little girl.

The summer before her first year of high school Meagan walked into the waters of baptism with her daddy by her side. This event seemed to bring about a quiet confidence as high school drew near and Meagan seemed to settle into a comfortable space with her friends, her basketball team, and the familiarity of school and church. Unbeknownst to us at the time, on her path, lay two events that would prove to one day significantly impact her life: A life-altering sports injury and the callous rejection of close friends. These two life experiences intertwined like weeds and barbed thickets that pulled her into their thick grasp.

During her high school years, Meagan received two severe concussions within fifteen months of each other that ended her sports career. The second occurred during her junior year of high school. From this point on, life would never be the same again. She could not attend a full day of class the rest of the school year and countless neurologist, neuropsychologist,

From this point on, life would never be the same again.

physical therapy, and tutoring appointments filled our day. She struggled with memory loss, confusion, headaches, balance issues and extreme sensitivity to sound. It would be a long road to recovery spiritually, physically, mentally, and emotionally.

Her diagnosis of Post-Traumatic Stress Disorder (PTSD) sent us through the typical stages of grief, denial, anger, sorrow, and eventually acceptance. Her neuropsychologist told us two things. First, she would face ridicule and people would eventually grow weary of what appeared to be a healing that took too long. Secondly, she told us we would see real changes in her personality and behaviors. We loved our energetic, loving Meg. We couldn't imagine losing the person we saw every day.

The neuropsychologist's words, however, became our reality. People did get tired of her and accused her of faking her behavior. Friends walked away, and she became more and more isolated. Her senior year was nothing like she thought it would be. She felt lost without basketball and struggled to find a place. She continued to experience severe and frequent headaches and had difficulty meeting the requirements of her classes, but managed to make it to graduation at the end of the school year. All the while I watched as she began to develop into someone much different than the daughter I had known. The closer graduation came, the greater our unspoken concern: *What would she do now?*

She felt confused and angry as she contemplated a future without basketball and no idea of what she wanted to do for a career. Her words tore at my heart, "I'm too stupid now for college. There's nothing for me here; I want to go back to Michigan." Three of the friends she had grown up with wanted Meagan to come for a visit. Good, reliable friends and a chance to have a new beginning would be an answer to prayer… or so we thought.

Her visit there would prove to be the moment she made a choice to lay her backpack of God-inspired tools down and wander off the path into the thickets and weeds. While in Michigan, Meagan's friends introduced her to alcohol and she liked it, way too much. She came home with a plan to move back to Michigan with a hidden motive to continue this behavior. Although she didn't know it at the time, Jesus never left her side. He was right there waiting for her to call out to him to rescue her and bring her back to His path.

She enrolled in beauty school and lived with close family friends. She started to go to the college ministry events at our old church and seemed to enjoy her new beauty school classes; she was back on familiar territory and poised for success. One day, about a month after her move back to Michigan, I awoke with an ominous feeling about Meagan. I gave her a call:

"Hello?" her shaky, weak voice answered.

Panic immediately rose inside of me, "Meg, what's going on? I haven't heard from you, and you don't sound good."

"Ummm…I'm okay? I just don't feel good."

"What do you mean you don't feel good, are you sick?" I asked.

After I prodded and poked, Meagan admitted she'd

drank way too much at a party the night before. She couldn't remember anything. She had woken up that morning in someone else's clothes, and there were blood stains on the pants.

My brain and heart crashed together. I struggled to make sense of what I had just heard. Trying not to let panic show in my voice, I asked, "Meagan, did someone do something to you?" (Please God please, let her say, "no!").

She said she couldn't remember much but that several of the girls had told her about two boys who entered a room where she lay on a bed, passed out. The girls said when they emerged from the room the boys bragged about what they had done to her.

After several phone calls and the scramble to make arrangements, I boarded a plane from St. Louis to Michigan. How would I ever find a way to make sense of what I had just heard and put the pieces of my heart, my daughter, and all of our lives back together again?

We spent the next week in meetings with a detective and quickly realized the battle of "he-said, she-said" would prevail. This was the beginning of the thickest entanglements in the thickets Meagan would experience. Instead of love and support, she received accusations and condemnations from her friends that this was all her fault. Instead of defending her, our somber detective showed up at the door at the end of the week to tell us there would be no case because there wasn't enough evidence to take the case to court. In Meagan's mind, she heard, "You're not worth fighting for." I wanted to draw Meagan in close and never let her out of my sight again.

Meagan tried over the next months to bring some order

to her life, but that was the problem: She hadn't grabbed hold of the hand of her Savior again because she was trying to restore her own life, the weeds and thickets overtook her once more. Her downward spiral into drinking and abuse was staggering. My husband and I could stand no more and decided to bring her back to St. Louis. She was only 20, but she was as worn as a woman who had lived three lifetimes.

Over the next year-and-a-half, Meagan spiraled farther down. She began to drink even more heavily and spend most of her time with unhealthy people. She became more and more angry with her family and distanced herself from us. We finally came to the place where we asked her to leave our home. In heart-broken tears, we told her we loved her, that God would always be by her side if she would just reach out to Him, and that when she was ready for actual change in her life, we would always be right here for her. Unfortunately, she continued to engage in the same self-destructive cycle of alcohol abuse, involvement with unhealthy people, and destructive men.

Meagan knew in the deepest part of her heart and soul that the Savior was waiting to take her hand, lead her back to His sure path, and help her to pick up her tools and backpack and continue on His triumphal way. But she wasn't ready yet. Instead, she turned to a man who proclaimed his love for her, but physically and emotionally abused her instead.

Several months later Meagan called, "Mom, I have something to tell you."

"Okay," my voice trembled, afraid of what I might hear next.

"My boyfriend and I broke up. We decided about a week ago to see less of each other to see if we would miss each other and then decide if we should stay together. The thing is, I didn't miss him, it was nice being away from him. I think God did that for me so I could see he isn't the one for me."

"Meg, I am so thankful you see how much God loves you. He's never going to leave you. He has a plan for your life; He's just waiting for you to ask Him for help," I said through tears.

Her response tore at my heart: "I know God can forgive me but why would he want to?"

It was the most authentic soul-revealing thing she'd said in months. She thought her sin too drastic and pervasive for God to want her back. Isn't that what most of us experience? We feel, erroneously, that what we have done is so unforgivable that Jesus' blood could never cover it. But, that's not true. Jesus' blood covers every sin.

> *God sent his Son into the world not to judge the world, but to save the world through him.* John 3:16, NLT

Later that same day tragedy struck. Her feelings of being unworthy to receive forgiveness and a celebrated life led to her to once again drink too much and take a handful of pills. A friend rushed her to the emergency room and then called me.

While Meagan may have been close to reaching out for her Rescuer's hand, there would be more weeds to entangle her before she fully intertwined her fingers with His. When I arrived at the emergency room, I looked at her as she lay unconscious while an IV pumped needed fluids into her body. The doctor and social worker asked me if I thought she was a danger to herself. I said, "Yes." I knew my answer put her in their hands; she would not be able to harm herself again.

Although she only spent 18 hours in their care, for the first time in a while Meagan's battered heart began to consider the possibility she could grab the hand of her Rescuer and return to His path for her. Over the next several weeks she readily accepted the restoring, healing words and gestures of wonderful people He was using as Hope-Markers to guide her back to Him.

Most importantly, she grabbed onto the hand of her Redeemer and didn't let go. With each day and each choice, she began to walk back to the path with Him, picking up her backpack and clinging to her map and compass, until one day she was able to say: "I know my past is a part of my story, but I'm not going to let it define who I am or who I will be."

At that moment, she seized her story and planted the final Hope-Marker of this part of her journey, marking the spot with a choice to move forward in God's identity, not the identity her experiences tried to impose on her. That choice has led her on a journey of planting new Hope-Markers of life-giving people and events: a loving husband, a beautiful new child, and a faith-filled community walking alongside her. She is an Overcomer.

Meagan chose to lay down her backpack with all of its tools and wander off into the thickets and weeds, which led her into a deep gorge. Jesus never left her, however, and waited for her to ask Him to help her. In her healing, He used each experience and each person as a Hope-Marker that guided her on her way. Life-giving experiences and the care of those who loved her became Hope-Markers as they inspired her to dive deeper into a relationship with her Savior. The painful people and experiences of her past became Hope-Markers of what she did not want for her future. Combined, her journey now includes the desire to become a Hope-Marker for others.

What about you? Whatever tragedy, pain, struggle, or heartache is in your past, God wants you to become an Overcomer. Your Hope-Markers will be those people and events that have both hurt and healed you. Both serve specific purposes: Painful ones are evidence of God's healing and serve as warning signs so we don't go into the weeds and life-giving ones are evidence of God's leadership in our lives, guiding us forward on His path.

Embrace your story by identifying the people and events that can guide you into your Rescuer's arms, marking your story with His hope. Your Hope-Markers will lead you through your own thickets and weeds back onto God's good path. The hurtful, painful experiences and people of your past can become Hope-Markers of change for you when you invite God in to heal you. Those who lovingly guide you, and the positive experiences you encounter, as a result, can become Hope-Markers of growth as you allow God to lead you through them. As you choose to pick up your backpack, your Hope-Markers, together with God's tools, will begin to guide you closer to Jesus who loves you, all of you, without fault. In that simple choice, each of us becomes an Overcomer.

CHAPTER SEVEN
The Redeemed: Olivia

The Savior not only helps the hurting become Overcomers, but he also redeems the hopeless. He generously offers his perfect gifts of both map and compass to every hopeless heart needing to be saved. He does this by going into the thickets and weeds to extend His hand to grasp and provide a backpack to guide them along the way. Olivia's story gives a picture of how the Savior pursues the hopeless and unabashedly offers to redeem their stories.

One steamy Sunday morning, as the hot summer sun beat on the large picture windows of the church where I worked, I looked about the lobby at those who entered. It was my job to welcome everyone and to make sure service went according to plan. Finishing up my duties as a guest relations staffer, I entered the auditorium and sat down next to my husband Ed who immediately and discreetly pointed over toward the front rows of the middle section of our sanctuary.

He leaned over next to my ear and, with urgency in his voice, he said, "See that girl over there? You need to go talk to her after service."

"You want me to go talk to who?" I asked.

He pointed over again to the middle section of chairs towards the front row. "The girl in the purple hoodie with the long dark hair. The one leaning over with her face in her hands. You need to go talk to her after service."

And then I saw her. She looked so sad, almost as if she was in pain. Was she grieving a loss? Was she trying to figure out God's plan for her? Did she even know how much The Father adored her?

I spent the rest of the service watching and praying for this wounded girl in the purple hoodie and long dark hair. As the service went on, she sank further into her chair and seemingly into a sea of hopelessness. Out of the corner of my eye, I watched as she cried softly with her head down and face buried.

The service ended, and most people began to file out of the auditorium, others stayed and visited with friends, and others went to the front to talk with a pastor. But not the girl in the purple hoodie; she sat paralyzed in her seat.

"I'll see you at home, I'll be praying for you as you talk with her," Ed said as he kissed me on the cheek.

Once again, I couldn't ignore the assurance that God planned this meeting with a girl He loved and wanted to be His own. Sitting down in a chair in the row of seats in front of her, I leaned over the back of the seat and smiled as I introduced myself.

"Hi, my name is Joan, and I am on staff here at the church. I hope you don't mind me saying but you look very sad. I want you to know that I was praying for you during the service."

She looked at me with red, blotchy, olive skin, and big tears in her eyes. She looked at me with such bleakness and said, "I. Am. So. Lonely."

At that moment, still unknown to her, she was making a choice to look up and reach out to Jesus for redemption. God had invited me to be used as a Hope-Marker and enter into this holy place with a beloved, broken-hearted child who so desperately needed to find hope in the Savior who desired to walk alongside her.

I asked her name, and she responded, "Olivia," with blandness in her voice. She went on to tell me that she was getting ready to start her senior year at a local university. Although guarded, she did open up enough to tell me that no matter how hard she tried to convince herself that she was worthy of love and authentic relationships, she just didn't believe it. We talked about counseling, and she said she had been going, but her biggest question centered on this idea of God's unconditional love, a love that could even be for her. Was it true? Could it heal her deep brokenness? Surely, she thought, she was the exception; she was just too broken.

After some time, we left the sanctuary and walked toward the lobby where I guided her to our bookstore. "Olivia, a group of about five of us are starting a book study this Tuesday. Would you like to join us? We would love to have you. It is very relaxed, a sort of come-as-you-are group for all of us."

Olivia stared at me with a look of disbelief. Her eyes seemed to question my trustworthiness; would I let her down and abandon her at some point like others in her life? I offered my cell number to her, which is not something I often do upon meeting someone for the first time, but it was apparent that God wanted her to have a lifeline so His powerful love could lead her out of the thickets and weeds. By the time she left, she had a copy of the book and directions for where we would meet. As she walked to her car, I noticed she was holding her head up for the first time since I'd met her. A Hope-Marker had been planted for her.

Later that night I received a text message from her that read, "I need you to know something. When they gave announcements and said that if we need to talk to someone we could come down front at the end of the service and speak with a pastor, I thought maybe I would try and do that when the service ended. Toward the end of the service, I just couldn't muster up the courage or the energy to go down. So I told God, 'If you are real and you love people the way they keep saying you do around here, then please send someone to talk to me because I'm not going up there.' I lifted my head, and you were sitting there."

At that moment, the Redeemer stood waiting to hand her a backpack filled with His tools. This Hope-Marker planting moment not only guided her future but mine as well. It reminds me never to pass up the opportunity that God gives to be the hands and feet of Jesus for a hurting loved one He places in my life.

That Tuesday night our group met and Olivia came. She listened intently, took notes, but didn't speak. It was all so new to her. For the first time, she considered the idea that there might be a backpack for her as we discussed God's goodness and desire for her to come close to Him. She struggled with worry and doubt; what if she didn't know how to use His Word and prayer (our compass and map) effectively? Would

At that moment, the Redeemer stood waiting to hand her a backpack filled with His tools.

that mean these things weren't for her? I assured her that these tools are for all of us, no matter how lost or confused we feel about using them. I told her that God desired to have a relationship with her and He knew her heart was open to him, regardless of how effectively she thought she was at prayer or understanding His word. A small ray of hope began to show through the thickets and weeds where the Savior had started to clear. For the first time, she considered the idea that things that seemed so strange – like hope, forgiveness, and healing – might really be for her. I invited her to our church's biggest event of the year that coming Sunday, our baptism celebration. Although I had to work at the event, I promised her we would spend time together.

Baptism Sunday was filled with organizing, activity, and holy moments where God transformed the lives of many. The event took place outside with hundreds of people, worship music, and opportunities for people to experience community. I prayed she would attend.

Late in the day, the buzz of my cell phone announced a text message. It was from her:

"I'm here. Can we still meet?"

As the heat faded and the sun began to set, we found a

spot on the curb of the parking lot. It had been a beautiful and holy day, and most people started to head home. We sat in silence for a while, just people watching. Scores of people had celebrated that Jesus had flooded their hearts with His tender love. This celebration was their testimony. Olivia seemed very curious about all of it.

"How do they all know? How do you know?" she asked with genuine curiosity.

I wasn't sure what she meant, and so I simply asked, "Know what?"

She continued, "How do you know all of this is true? I heard people talk today about the life of sin they lived before knowing Jesus; about the struggles and hurt they had experienced before they trusted the Rescuer to save them. Now they are set free? What does that mean? God could never forgive me. I'm a throw-away."

"Olivia, those are big questions," I replied. "I can't promise you I have all of the answers, but we will walk this together and find them. The one thing I can tell you right now is that everything you heard tonight is true. He is an adoring Father, and He wants to rescue you from your hurt and pain. I know it's real because He did the same for me."

We spent the next hour unraveling her story. Olivia spent the first 2 years of her life in an orphanage in Romania. Then a family from Canada adopted her. A large part of her sadness stemmed from the fact that she was grieving, but she didn't know who or what to grieve. How could she ever get past what she did not know? She also moved quite a bit as a child, which further added to her inability to know how to form relationships or really receive or give affection. She lost herself in sports, schooling and anything else that could distract her from the grief, loss of identity and the lies telling her she was unworthy of love. She later said that it was just easier to make up her own God because she didn't like the God she had been introduced to as a child; a disconnected, judgmental God who was uninvolved in her life. By creating her own God, she could dish out her own forms of punishment and coping methods.

She pushed herself academically, only accepting the best grades. Athletically, she went beyond reasonable workouts, all while she binged and purged, hoping the weight loss would give her an edge. Then, when she couldn't handle the heavy load of guilt and self-hatred, she cut herself and dove into unhealthy relationships. She hit rock-bottom when she received two concussions that ended her athletic career; yet another failure that only made her more unlovable. She was seeing a counselor for her self-destructive behavior, but it wasn't getting to the core of her soul as the person God created her to be. She felt completely immobilized by the thickets and weeds of her life.

She let me pray for her, and we agreed to meet again. We made plans for her to begin to meet other people at the church; a pastor, a friend who was a counselor, and other women who I knew would encourage her. Since Meagan had also fought through her own battle of concussions that ended a sports career I thought it would be good for Olivia to hear her story as well. Meagan had come to embrace the Father's love for her; her past was a part of her story, but it didn't define her. Olivia could come to this place as well.

Olivia slowly began to trust me and those I introduced her to. More importantly, she began to consider that there might be a backpack with influential tools for her. Early on in our conversations, she shared with me that she had no friends, no one in her life. Over time, God had placed other believers in her life, but she did not connect with them; they remained only in her peripheral. The women around her now, however, would prove to be instrumental in her transformation.

We continued to have big conversations about what an audacious revolutionary Jesus was when he lived on Earth. We talked about how He came to break through the chains of performance, guilt, and shame to create a new culture of loving even the unlovely, the minimized and the forgotten. We worked through the false notion that she had to somehow make herself presentable before she could go to the Father to receive His saving grace. One day, about three months later, she called me on the phone with big news.

"I'm ready!" she said. "I'm not sure what this will all look like, and I'm a little bit scared, but tonight my roommate and I are going to pray. I want what Jesus did for me to fill me up; I want to know more and more the love of the Father."

She had decided to meet with a friend that night to pray and take the hand of the Savior who would set her on a sure path she could travel with Him on an adventurous journey.

I told her I would pray for her throughout that day. Later that evening she sent me a video. There stood Olivia in front of a campfire holding a red helium balloon. With tears in her eyes, she looked up into the dark starry sky and said,

"Jesus, this balloon represents all the hurt, pain, and sin in my life. I'm letting it go and turning it all over to you. I can't do life anymore without you. Be my Savior. I also pray that Father you would continue to show me your love. I don't completely understand it yet, but I know you're real."

Then she released the balloon and watched it float up into

the night sky. She finally turned toward the person recording with the biggest smile I had ever witnessed on her face. I was undone.

That night one of her most influential Hope-Markers was planted as she connected with Jesus for all eternity.

Olivia continued to experience great victories over the next months as she grew in the knowledge of the love of God. She attended church, soaked in messages of love, participated in study groups, and leaned into God-honoring relationships. Her backpack of God's influential tools became her most prized possession as she poured through scripture and wrestled with God in prayer over her big questions. She also worked with God and other journey-women to plant other Hope-Markers in her life as she learned to recognize that struggles, temptations, and discouragement sometimes meets us on our journey; but with His tools, she could receive healing and stay connected to the Savior.

Olivia and I would attend another Baptism Sunday together. This time, Olivia entered the waters of baptism and publicly declared she no longer lived in the thickets and weeds. She had become one of the redeemed.

Hopelessness had marked Olivia's past due to loneliness, because in her words:

"I intentionally closed myself off. I built walls around myself and didn't let anyone in because I was hurting so badly I didn't want anyone near me, or I might be hurt and abandoned more. When you build walls you sit in your isolation wondering how you will ever break free. I wanted to be rescued but I didn't know how to get the message outside of the walls."

When she was ready, however, she called out, ready

He reached in, tore through the thickets and weeds she was entangled in and set her firmly on His journey of redemption.

to break free, and the Rescuer came. He reached in, tore through the thickets and weeds she was entangled in and set her firmly on His journey of redemption. She has seized her story and now the events of her past and the people that God had placed on her path have now become a source of Hope-Markers in her life. Like Meagan, her identity will not be found in her painful, lonely past. She has chosen to allow the hope of her future to identify her instead.

No matter what thickets or weeds you are in the middle of, God wants to rescue you too and place you firmly on His path of hope. You are not lost to Him. He is right there with you no matter how hopeless you feel or how desperate your situation looks. You need only make a choice to look up and reach out; His hand will be there to grasp yours. As you do, He will place your backpack, equipped with His map and compass, gently upon your shoulders:

> *Come to me, all of you who are weary and burdened, and I will give you rest. Take my yoke upon you. Let me teach you because I am humble and gentle at heart, and you will find rest for your souls. For my yoke is easy to bear, and the burden I give you is light.* Matthew 11:28-30, NLT

Once you are steady, He will begin the journey with you of planting Hope-Markers in your life. He will take the pain and struggle of your past and offer His healing. He will plant his Hope-Markers and use them to guide you into life-giving relationships and experiences meant to draw you closer in relationship with Him. With Him, you too can become Redeemed.

> *You are not lost to Him. He is right there with you no matter how hopeless you feel or how desperate your situation looks.*

CHAPTER EIGHT

The World Changer: Stephanie

We've been on a journey that ultimately leads to living the life of a World-Changer. A World-Changer is someone who has humbled themselves before God, embraced their story, and then encourages others to do the same by teaching them to use the Hope-Markers in their lives.

When God calls us to live the life of a World-Changer, it doesn't mean it will be easy. It takes intentional effort to allow God to call forth the events and people from our past and to shape them into Hope-Markers that empower us. We can then use that empowerment to impact the world. My friend Stephanie is a model of one who became a World-Changer by drawing in close to the Father, recognizing the Hope-Markers of her past, and using them to empower change for herself, her family, and the world around her.

> *A World-Changer is someone who has humbled themselves before God, embraced their story, and then encourages others to do the same by teaching them to use the Hope-Markers in their lives.*

There was a time in Stephanie's life where she seemed to do it all. She wore many hats – wife, mother, writer, teacher, speaker, volunteer, sports fan, and the list goes on. At one point in her life, she allowed the messiness of her constant striving to take over who she knew herself to be as a daughter of the King. She let go of God's hand in the quest to try and be Wonder Woman. It's as if she said, "I love you, God, just let me go fix ____________ and I'll be right back."

To those who were watching Stephanie, they would tell you she did a pretty good job at being Wonder Woman. At first, the cracks appeared so lightly on the surface of Stephanie's Wonder Woman suit that someone talking with her barely noticed the perfection crumbling. The consistency with which she consulted her map and her compass grew less and less as the pressure mounted.

Then one day I got a phone call from Stephanie. She was discouraged and disillusioned. God had begun to call her to a place of solitude where she would spend time with Him and give up her hectic schedule.

"For the next six months, God is calling me to just 'be.' No speaking engagements, no extra activities. I'm just going to spend time with Him," she said with some trepidation of what that might look like.

The Wonder Woman costume had come off. During this period of "just being" instead of "doing," there were times of deep connection with God where together they looked at events and people from her past that marked her story. As she went back through her story, she allowed Him to heal her hurts, and looked for the Hope-Markers she could use to make her path clearer. She once again picked up her map and compass and held onto them firmly as she walked the path God was calling her to for a renewed future of planting Hope-Markers for herself and others. This is the point where Stephanie truly became a World-Changer.

Stephanie came out of those six months renewed, focused, and energized. She began to embrace God's calling fully, and it showed. She re-prioritized her life making Him and His plans front and center. With His plan before her, she embarked on the journey of a World-Changer.

The dynamic part of being a World-Changer is that it looks different in each of us. To release ourselves to God in this way can be a little scary. When we are used to operating in a mode of constant chaos and striving, it takes an intentional heart to release it to God, take His hand again and let Him lead. When we find ourselves at that scary place of releasing there are three principles from scripture that can lead us:

- Humble ourselves before God and His plan
- Embrace our story as an influential tool to guide our steps
- Encourage and equip others to be World-Changers

We all come to crossroads in our walk with God and we must make a choice as to which path we will follow. One path continues on the same we have come. It's marked with busy schedules, bills to pay, appointments to keep, be sure to check Sunday church services off the list… and the "to do's" go on. None of these things are bad in and of themselves, but when they absorb our thoughts, our emotional health, and the peace in our hearts, we have made them our markers of what gives us value and purpose in life. It's a rocky, unsure path that eventually crumbles under our feet because we can't keep up with all the demands on our own strength.

This is the place on the path that Stephanie found herself: At the crossroads. The Wonder Woman path where she did everything with her own strength, became rocky and filled with pot holes and had begun to crumble under her. It was too treacherous to continue to follow. The first option was to continue on that path.

The second path of the crossroads is one of "just being." It is a way of humbly surrendering to God's ways. It leads to the world-changing life God calls all of us to live. It starts with a conscious choice to stop where we are and humbly go to God in prayer and His Word to ask for His direction and calling; staying quiet long enough to listen until

Trust Him enough to let Him change the trajectory of your life and put you on the path of the World-Changer.

God calls us to take the next step. This mindset calls for a complete trust in God.

Maybe you're saying "just being" isn't possible for you right now. Unfortunately, you don't have the option of cutting off your hectic schedule to "just-be" for six months because the demands on you are too great. Maybe you're a single mom or are the breadwinner of your family, or you're caring for an aging parent. Let me encourage you by telling you God already knows that. He sees all of the responsibility on you. Go to Him. Tell Him all of this. Let Him speak to your heart in that still quiet voice that is filled with love, compassion, and truth only a Father can give His children. Trust Him enough to let Him change the trajectory of your life and put you on the path of the World-Changer.

He may not call you to take six months, but He will ask you to take time to hear what He has to say to stay firmly planted on His path. This time looks different for us all. For some, it may mean spending time on a daily walk in the woods having a conversation with Him. For others, it means daily sitting in a comfy chair with a cup of coffee and your Bible. The point is to be intentional about quieting our hearts, souls, and minds so we can hear the purpose of God's will for our journey. It may take some time to hear, but there is growth in the quiet if we take the time to stay there. There will be a point when His direction for you will become apparent. Don't fret about how long it will take. He has perfect timing and He will direct you where he wants you to go.

No matter what it looks like in our lives, we all need to take time to "just be." During this period, we find an opportunity to prepare ourselves for real dependence on God's plan:

> *For whoever exalts himself will be humbled, and whoever humbles himself will be exalted.* Matthew 23:12, The Voice

Humble

Humility allows us the freedom to embrace all of our stories and then trust God to take control. We have the freedom to embrace the story God has instead of bending to the way the world says we should live. When we humble ourselves before Him, we are ready to take the next steps of being a World-Changer.

The humbling of our souls and minds is revolutionary in a world of self-promotion. If we truly humble ourselves before God, self-promotion is not necessary. He will do the lifting up and exalting. It is a holy give-and-take. We humble ourselves before God, waiting in submission for Him to reveal His plan and He affirms us in His work. Then, others are blessed through the process because the real message of God reaches them through our God-ordained ministry.

Embrace

During Stephanie's furlough, she spent time asking God to help her embrace her story and establish the Hope-Markers in her life. She asked for help remembering that her past failings had already been taken to the cross. She sought God's direction to create healthy boundaries and allowed God to decide who would be let in and who could no longer capture her heart or thought life. Her future promised to be God-inspired, as she walked more closely on her path holding His hand tighter and keeping her eyes on Him and not on anyone else.

She now knows she would not have been able to write her book or minister to others in such a God-honoring way if she had not grasped who she is and what her story has to tell. She has allowed God to show her how to embrace her story so that now it is defined by His glory. Her story no longer defined her.

Many of us not only struggle with trying to be Wonder Woman but also with moments of feeling unimportant. We may think we have "ordinary" stories that can't have an impact on others. We minimize who we are by saying things like, "I'm just a mom," or "I never went to college," or "I'm not in a position of leadership or influence." We need to choose to walk away from these lies that entangle and keep us hopelessly wandering.

David wrote in Psalms,

Praise the Lord, my soul, and forget not all his benefit – who forgives all your sins and heals all your diseases, who redeems your life from the pit and crowns you with love

and compassion, who satisfies your desires with good things so that your youth is renewed like the eagle's
(Psalm 103: 2-5, NIV)

These are the words of a man who learned to embrace his story, both the ugliness of his sin and the tragedy of what had happened to him, and see it through the map and compass of God's healing of his past and victorious path-walking in his present and future. Notice the last part of this verse. Through David's repentance, forgiveness, and healing, his youth was "renewed." According to Holman's Treasury of Key Bible Words,[4] the Hebrew word for renewed is Chadesh and it means to "repair or to restore."

This is what happens when we lock hands with God on our path walking and embrace our story. He repairs and restores our past circumstances both emotionally and spiritually and turns those moments into Hope-Markers. We stop minimizing who we are because of these conditions, because we are renewed and ready to be all He is calling us to be in our present and future. Our repaired and restored stories are the natural result of story seizing and we can then become an inspiration for others to be World-Changers.

Encourage and Equip

Emboldened by our story-seizing experiences, God calls us to walk alongside other women, helping them see God's way off the rocky twists and turns of life-striving on our

---

[4] Holman Illustrated Bible Dictionary. (2003). Holman Bible Publishers, Nashville, Tennessee.

own. We become more in tune with others to experience "Me too!" moments so we can connect and draw in close to other journey-women using our Hope-Markers.

Stephanie seized opportunities to connect relationally with those around her so they would know they were much more than what they were telling themselves. She used her book to help women find peace in the midst of daily chaos. She met with them, prayed with them, and allowed them to speak into her life as well. Stephanie's ministry began to flourish as she encouraged and equipped others to do what she had done: humble themselves before God, embrace His impact on their stories and take His hand for the next steps of their journeys.

Stephanie encouraged and equipped other women to move along their path of becoming World-Changers. They weren't necessarily called to write books or speak at events. They became World-Changers by using their own stories in the way God called them to on their unique journey. They set out on their world-changing by becoming volunteers at their children's local school. They mentored other women at work. They championed a friend dealing with a serious illness. They loved their husbands well. The underlying message changed from the busyness of life to a call of God on their lives to have Him author their story in the future instead of trying to write it themselves, as they had in the past.

As World-Changers, we have the potential to affect our "small world," meaning our immediate sphere of influence. Once a person faithfully encourages and equips others, the effects move beyond their "small world." Those who have learned to humble themselves before God and encourage and equip others in the ways of God begin to connect with others.

Our stories all look different. The influence of sharing our stories spreads beyond our "small world" as each woman's story, in turn, is woven together into an ever-increasing network of encouragement and empowerment.

While imprisoned, Paul wrote a letter to Philemon, a man who was known for his faithful sharing of the gospel. Paul encourages him to continue his work of inspiring others with the message of God:

> *Thank you father, for Philemon. I pray that as he goes and tells his story of faith, he would tell everyone so that they will know for certain all the good that comes to those who put their trust in the Anointed one.* Philemon 1:6, The Voice

Although it is clear that Philemon inspired his "small world," he now moved beyond to impact the "big world'" because he inspired those beyond his sphere of influence. We too can be "small-world" inspirers and "big-world" inspirers. Inspiring beyond our "small world" can take many forms. After all, we have a creative Father God who desires to use our story to impact others. How many times have we been on some form of social media and read a story about a woman battling cancer and how she has inspired her friends and family so much that they are motivated to put her story out there for us all to see? They champion, pray, and ask others to pray for them. The woman battling cancer is a World-Changer because she has inspired others to goodness and generous giving of self.

In the physical world most would see their lives as ordinary, but in the supernatural world in which God operates,

We all have the potential to inspire others to become "big-world" changers. Why? Because we are loved by a God who thinks we are important to the world and He knows our stories matter and can be used in someone else's life.

they are anything but ordinary. In God's world, each story is a powerful tool for fighting off the enemy and meant to propel each of us ahead into the future victoriously with Him. Our stories become Hope-Markers; markers that can show fearless warriors battling in prayer for someone else. And others of inspiring mentors who are humble enough to say they may not have it all together, but feel called to walk along with someone not quite as far along the path as they are.

We all have the potential to inspire others to become "big-world" changers. Why? Because we are loved by a God who thinks we are important to the world and He knows our stories matter and can be used in someone else's life. The possibilities are endless.

When we truly seek after that plan and spend time in preparation for the journey, we will be ready for whatever He calls us to. When we use our map and compass with our Hope-Markers, we are equipped with the tools necessary to live out the life of a World-Changer. It will not be the same path as someone else; as He has a tailor-made plan just for you because you are worth it and you have a story to tell. Wait patiently for his calling on what He is asking you to do. He holds the universe in the balance and he knows how and when your story will best achieve His purposes and help you to become a World-Changer.

CHAPTER NINE

Living Hope-Markers

If you've read up to this point and you're thinking you have a long way to go to being a world changer, you're not alone. The process of seizing your story, identifying your Hope-Markers, and ultimately beginning to change the world around you, is ongoing. All of us have areas of our lives we make quick progress and struggle to achieve even baby steps in others. The key is to keep your eyes focused on Jesus.

Another thing to remember is that while we are working on identifying the Hope-Markers in our lives, we can become Hope-Markers for others. We can be an "Angela" to someone not as far down the faith path as we are and encourage them along. Mentoring someone is a wonderful way to become a Hope-Marker and world-changer. It may sound intimidating at first but when you begin to mentor someone, you realize it's just a relationship with a purpose. An eternal purpose. I leave you with this quote from Beth Moore:

> You cannot amputate your history from your destiny, because that is redemption."[5]

The key is to keep your eyes focused on Jesus.

[5] Beth Moore, Esther: It's Tough Being a Woman, [With 6 DVDs and Leader Guide, Member Book] November 1, 2008 by Lifeway Christian Resource

HOPE MARKERS

Study Guide

Note from the Author

I am so glad we are walking this journey hand-in-hand with Jesus. This study guide is my way of saying, "We are in this together!" It is designed to help you know that your story matters, your Hope-Markers matter, you matter. God wants you to embrace this truth because you are His daughter, He loves you, and He is pleased with you.

My prayer is that this study guide will be a tool to aid you as you travel the journey of becoming a World-Changer. He desires for you to see yourself as one of His Redeemed Overcomers. When we embrace this truth about who we are in him we can share this message first in our "small world" and then inspire the "big world."

There are three sections of questions for the introduction and all nine chapters:

Reflection:

These questions are designed for your own intimate time with God. They have been crafted to help you embrace your story, mark your present and future with Hope-Markers, and become the World-Changer God designed you to be.

Discussion:

We all need time to unpack our stories with other journey-women. The discussion questions will help guide your conversation and help you encourage one another as you dig deeper into God's purpose for your journey.

Action:

The fruition of our reflection and discussion is played out in how our daily life is transformed. These points and challenges assist you in taking action to journey alongside Jesus to change the trajectory of your present and future.

Please note: These questions can be intertwined into other section questions. You may find that you are with a safe group and desire to answer some of the reflection questions in your discussion with others. Action steps and discussion questions can be answered during your reflection time. I encourage you to take full advantage of using the questions how God leads you to do so.

Thank you for traveling this journey with me. I am deeply humbled that you have made Hope-Markers apart of your journey with God. I would love to hear from you! Please feel free to share your story with me by contacting me on my website: www.joangallagher.net.

Introduction

Reflection:

As of today, which bricklayer do you most identify with in your life?

Is there a person or event from your past that immediately comes to mind when you think of how your life has been influenced? Is it a cause for hope for your future or one of trepidation?

Discussion:

"This book is intended to help you identify the markers of the past to better understand your present and impact the trajectory of your future." What is your first reaction when you hear the words "fear, excitement, anxiety." Explain your answer.

Action:

"Ultimately, we can come to a place of holding up those Hope-Markers as triumphal reflections to others, using our influence to help change the world one story at a time." Spend some time considering what it means for you to use your story to influence change in the world. What would this practically look like? What emotions does it stir up for you? Spend time in prayer with the Father considering what this means for you.

Chapter 1: Your Story Matters

Reflection:

What was the last conversation you remember sharing a vulnerable part of your story? Was the other person willing to share the sensitive parts of their story? If so how did this sharing impact your relationship? (Note: If it is hard to remember a time you had this kind of conversation, begin to pray for God's leading in finding authentic relationships and to be more open in sharing your story with a trusted woman of God.)

What lies about you from the past are you still holding on to in your present? What lies have you overcome through the power of God in your life?

Do you see God moving in your story? How or why not?

Discussion:

What do you think God sees when he looks at you?

Romans 12: 2 says, "Do not be conformed to this world, but be transformed by the renewal of your mind, that by testing you may discern what is the will of God, what is good and acceptable and perfect" (NIV). How does this verse speak to a renewed future in your life?

Have you ever had a "Me too!" moment with someone? Explain.

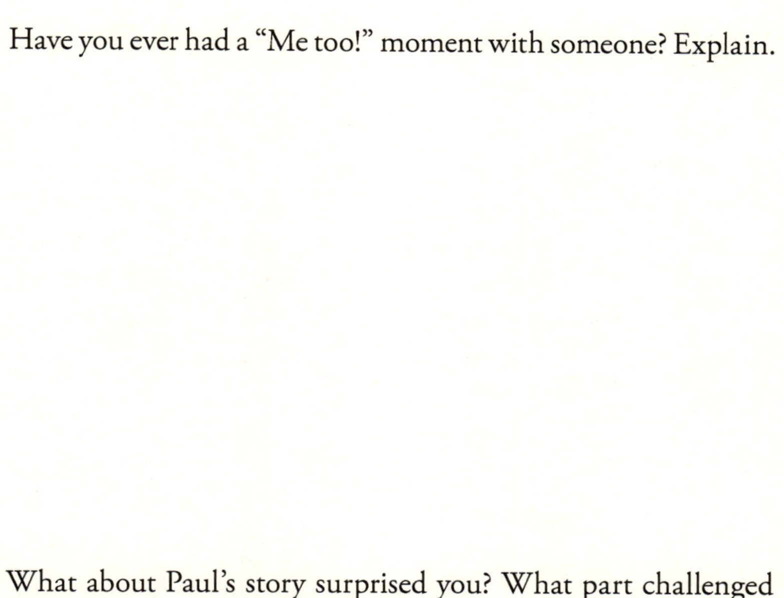

What about Paul's story surprised you? What part challenged you? What part encouraged you?

Action:

Take some time to consider this big thought: "The story of our life matters. It matters first and foremost because we matter to God. He loves us and desires to heal our hurts and show us how the struggles we encounter have lessons in them to benefit us. No matter what the pain of our stories contains, when God comes in, we can receive healing." What does this mean for you and how you see your own story? Try writing it down, and in prayer commit your future story to His work.

Where are you on the path of having a transformed life? Have you allowed God to do His work of healing your past? If not where does this begin for you? If so what does this part of your story look like? Begin to cultivate your story so that God may use it to encourage others.

Chapter 2: Hope-Markers

Reflection:

Have you felt the stinging sentiments of "Unclean!" flung at you? How have you dealt with this in the past? Have you trusted in the power of hope in Jesus Christ to bring about healing for you?

"When we choose to mark our stories, we transform our lives. No longer does our story define us with such labels as 'unclean,' 'inconsequential,' 'useless,' or whatever other labels is shoved at us by the enemy. Instead, our stories are used as markers to guide the trajectory that God is calling us to follow." What labels do you need freed from? What markers of truth does God want you to hear?

"When we learn to use Hope-Markers in our lives, the outcome of this connectedness with Jesus Christ is a present filled with peace, a future poised to flourish, and an opportunity to point others to the same connection with the great God of love." What does this kind of living look like for you?

Discussion:

Where do you place your hope for change in areas of your life?

Describe what you think the woman with the bleeding issue felt at the moment of healing?

Action:

Begin to identify the Hope-Markers in your life. Who were people who influenced your life, both positive and negative? What events in your life have impacted your story?

"We can look for Hope-Markers in our story by asking ourselves a few key questions:

> When did we put our full hope in God to walk our journey with us?
>
> What event/s led us to a deeper trust in His will for us?
>
> Who did God place in our life to stretch us, or lead us, or was used by God to rescue us?"

Try journaling your answers to these questions.

Chapter 3: How Hope Marks Your Story

Reflection:

"Why am I overwrought? Why am I so disturbed? Why can't I just hope in God? Despite all my emotions, I will believe and praise the One who saves me and is my life" (Psalm 42:5, The Voice). Do you sense the tension between the first three sentences of this verse and the last? Have you felt yourself in this place before?

Like the woman with the bleeding issue, was there a moment for your that changed the trajectory of your life? Have you used this moment to inspire the lives of others?

Discussion:

How do you see Hope-Markers changing your story?

Share a situation from your path when you felt overwhelmed and how that same situation can look differently when seen it through God's lens?

What parts of your story have you embraced? What parts are you struggling to embrace?

Action:

In your journey, begin to consider a Hope-Marker in your life that God can use to continue to guide you on your path.

Remind yourself every day, "My story matters because I matter to God."

Chapter 4: Pack Your Backpack

Reflection:

How much are you relying on your map (the Bible) and compass (Prayer) to guide your life?

"Simply put, prayer is the time we spend with our heavenly Father. He wants us to get to know Him so He can show us that our story matters to Him." What does prayer look like to you?

What person or event do you need to begin to see as a Hope-Marker by interweaving it with your map and compass?

Discussion:

Do you have an "Angela" in your life who was or is a Hope-Marker that helped you along your journey?

How do you encounter God in His Word and in prayer?

How do you see your map and compass working in conjunction with your Hope-Markers to lead you on your journey with God? Provide an example of how this is true for you.

Action:

Make a point to be more intentional about your time with God. What is hindering you? Take it before God and be creative in finding ways to connect? Is it a walk in nature or finding a favorite spot in your house? Maybe it's just a matter of getting up 15 minutes earlier to spend time with Him.

Spend time over the next week praying and writing the Lord's prayer:

> *Our Father in heaven,*
> *hallowed be your name,*
> *your kingdom come,*
> *your will be done,*
> *on earth as it is in heaven.*
> *Give us today our daily bread.*
> *And forgive us our debts,*
> *as we also have forgiven our debtors.*
> *And lead us not into temptation,*
> *but deliver us from the evil one* (NIV).

After you have done this, write this prayer in your own words; that is, how God is leading you to pray.

Use the space below to write The Lord's Prayer in your own words:

Chapter 5: Seize your Story

Reflection:

Are you allowing your story to hurt you more than help you? What thoughts and feelings about your story are you allowing to persuade your actions?

During the struggles of weeds and thickets consider the fact that Jesus loves you and that we can't travel this journey without Him.

What Hope-Marker serves as a reminder of how God redeemed a part of your story?

Discussion:

"Story seizing begins the very moment we invite God into the heart-wrestling of our stories so He can define the trajectory of our present and future." What "heart-wrestling" do you need to invite the Divine Definer so He can influence the trajectory of your present and future?

Share a time when you allowed yourself to wonder into the thickets and weeds of this world and how the Rescuer brought you back to the path to travel with Him.

"If God is silent, He has a purpose to do so that is for our benefit. He may be asking us to wait right at the place we are on our path. God is not calling us to an inactive period. On the contrary, He is calling us to pursue Him in prayer and in His Word in patient expectancy for His plan to unfold." What does this period of waiting look like for you? Do you spend it in prayer, His Word and in patient expectancy? If not what needs to change for you?

Action:

Spend some time journaling what it looks like for you to seize your story, your heart-wrestling. Then use your map (the Bible) and compass (Prayer) to see what God says about these things and how he wants to influence your story.

Pray for and seek out God-honoring relationships so that you can spend time unpacking your story with a trusted mentor. Focus on learning about each other's Hope-Markers and how they can influence your journey.

Chapter 6: Hope-Marking Case Study 1
The Overcomer

Reflection:

Is there a specific event from your past that caused an unexpected tragic change to the trajectory of your life? What were the messages that you heard spoken to your heart and soul?

Is there a part of your story that was the moment you became an Overcomer?

Discussion:

"Her visit there would prove to be the moment she made a choice to lay her backpack of God-inspired tools down and wander off the path into the thickets and weeds." Meagan's turning point came when she acknowledged that she had laid down her backpack. If this is true for you as well, recall a time when you laid down your backpack and the moment you picked it back up again.

Name a Hope-Marker whether a person (**I encourage you to not use the names of others when naming a negative impact in your life) or event that caused you to invite God in to heal you.

Do you have a desire to be a Hope-Marker in someone else's life? What do you think that would look like for you based on your own experiences?

Action:

In an earlier chapter we talked about the importance of heart-wrestling. We find Meagan at this point in her story when she made the statement, "I know God can forgive me but why would he want to?" What is your heart-wrestling moment?

Now take that moment and search God's Word and spend time with Him in prayer to better understand this moment.

Then, acknowledge this time as a Hope-Marker in which God wants to us to change the trajectory of your life. Embrace it, plant it, and celebrate what God will do through this moment.

It can take some time to do this embracing, planting and celebrating. I encourage you to travel this part of your path with someone who can walk alongside of you and guide you through this time. Become an Overcomer.

Chapter 7: Hope-Marking Case Study 2
The Redeemed

Reflection:

Recall a time when you realized God stood waiting, offering His hand to lead you out of the weeds and thickets. Spend time in thanksgiving to God, acknowledging His faithfulness in your life.

Come to me, all of you who are weary and burdened, and I will give you rest. Take my yoke upon you. Let me teach you because I am humble and gentle at heart, and you will find rest for your souls. For my yoke is easy to bear, and the burden I give you is light Matthew 11:28-30, NIV.

Spend time memorizing these verses. What do they mean to you? Use them as a marker to guide you on your journey; in particular, when you feel weary. Remind yourself that He is the perfect guide in challenging times.

Discussion:

Share the moment that God redeemed your hopeless heart and offered you His hand and His backpack to walk your journey with Him.

Olivia had big God questions she wanted to wrestle with as she grew in her faith. What big God questions do you wrestle with?

How has God used some of His people to play a pivotal part in your journey?

Action:

"It reminds me never to pass up the opportunity that God gives to be the hands and feet of Jesus for a hurting loved one He places in my life."

Begin to pray for and look for opportunities to be the hands and feet of Jesus for someone else in their story. You will become a Hope-Marker for them.

Write and cultivate your story of becoming God's own, His Redeemed, so that you can share with others all He has done for you.

Chapter 8: Hope-Marking Case Study 3
The World Changer

Reflection:

"A World-Changer is someone who has humbled themselves before God, embraced their story, and then encourages others to do the same by teaching them to use the Hope-Markers in their lives." Have you embraced the life of a World-Changer? If not what holds you back from embracing this truth?

During your time to "just be," what are the hurts you need to take to God, and what Hope-Markers can be used by God to make your path clearer?

What one word would you use to describe your story – ordinary, adventurous, painful, redeemed? Be honest with yourself and see what God needs to change in you.

Discussion:

"'For the next six months, God is calling me to just 'be.' No speaking engagements, no extra activities. I'm just going to spend time with Him,' she said with some trepidation of what that might look like.'" Your time to "just be" will look different than Stephanie's. What might this look like for you?

What does it look like for you to be a World-Changer?

David wrote in Psalms, "Praise the LORD, my soul, and forget not all his benefits—who forgives all your sins and heals all your diseases, who redeems your life from the pit and crowns you with love and compassion, who satisfies your desires with good things so that your youth is renewed like the eagle's" (Psalm 103:2-5, NIV). David learned to embrace His story and he was renewed. This is the story of a story-seizer. Have you seized your story? What parts of your story have you embraced and what parts still need God's renewing?

Action:

Spend time intentionally humbling yourself in prayer to God. Wait submissively in prayer before Him, allowing Him to speak. Submission takes intentionality. Offer yourself to Him for whatever He has for you and see what God will do.

Begin to consider how your Hope-Markers might help to encourage and equip others. Write them down and practice telling these stories to a trusted friend.

Look for "Me too!" moments with those you encounter. When we do, we find opportunities to impact our "small world," as well as inspire our "big world." We can then have said of us what Paul said of Philemon: "Thank you father, for Philemon. I pray that as he goes and tells his story of faith, he would tell everyone so that they will know for certain all the good that comes to those who put their trust in the Anointed one" Philemon 1:6, The Voice.

Chapter 9: Living Hope-Markers

Reflection:

Today, do you feel alone in the process of seizing your story?

Reflect on how changing your mindset to plant Hope-Markers can change the trajectory of your present and future.

Discussion:

"The process of seizing your story, identifying your Hope-Markers, and ultimately beginning to change the world around you is ongoing." What is your reaction to the point that the Hope-Marker process is ongoing? Do you feel encouraged or intimidated? Explain your answer.

Have you had an instrumental mentor in your life? Have you been a mentor to someone else? How can the Hope-Markers concept aid you in a mentoring relationship?

Action:

In the morning, before you even get out of bed, ask God to help you keep your eyes focused on Him that day.

Look for opportunities to be an "Angela" in someone else's life.

Women Mentoring Women

Women Mentoring Women is dedicated to empowering women to use their God-inspired stories to build healthy mentoring relationships. When we allow each other into our stories we give opportunity to experience community, invite wisdom, know healing, and embrace the tender powerful love of Jesus.

Sign up on the website and join the community of women who are sharing their stories, building God-centered relationships, and living out the hope for a celebrated present and future.

At www.joangallagher.net, you will find a landing place to help you further your opportunities to embrace your story and cultivate relationships with other women. You will be able to read other women's stories and Christ-centered messages through my blog posts. You'll also find up-to-date information such as:

- A FREE guide to effectively travel the path of embracing your story and becoming a World-Changer. This helpful companion to each chapter of Hope-Markers shares thought provoking questions and encouragements to enrich your storytelling and relationship building.

- A sneak peak of my next book. Hint: It's all about relationship building and the power of mentoring!

- Opportunities for free giveaways such as reliable resources to aid you on your journey.

I would love to hear from you! Contact me through my website or by emailing me and let me know your story and how Hope-Markers has impacted your journey. Please sign up on the website to receive newsletters, the latest blogs, and updates about my next project and how you can be a part.

www.joangallagher.net
joan.gallagher.nowo@gmail.com

Excerpt from:

The Call of Hope: How to Find Passionate Relationships Through Mentoring

(*working title*)

We love because He first loved us.
1 John 4:19, NIV

It's clear from 1 John 4 that John was passionate about the love God has for us. He shows us how God invented and then models this revolutionary idea: pouring love into our relationships should FIRST come from a place of receiving love. God's love. When the perfect love from our heavenly Father stirs in our hearts and souls it pours out passionate, heart-serving relationships with others.

One of the areas of our lives where this "pouring out" can be life-changing is in a mentoring relationship. The relationship between a mentor and her mentee is a perfect opportunity to exhibit the kind of love God calls us to have for one another. The call to love authentically and from a place of first receiving love is the absolute foundation of the mentoring relationship.

There are two ways a mentor can inspire a mentee to "love like God." The first is an intentional sharing of life experience. Our stories are a rich source of what I like to call Hope-Markers. These Hope-Markers are places where God steps into our story to plant His hope in our lives. They can include both encouraging people and experiences as well as those that drain us spiritually, mentally, and physically. As well as the planting of God's Word in our hearts and lives. Through the guiding of the Holy Spirit, we can offer the wisdom we have gained as a result of sharing the stories behind the planting of these Hope-Markers.

The second way a mentor can inspire a mentee to love like God in her relationships is through using her wisdom to help her mentee live out God's call on her life. Teaching a mentee to fill her spiritual backpack with her compass (prayer) and her map (God's Word), gives each mentee a solid foundation from which to take her next steps of faith. This part of the mentoring relationship often looks more like facing life's situations together through diving into God's word for guidance, praying for wisdom from the Spirit, and encouraging our mentee to trust God with her next steps.

With God as the center, the mentoring relationship is now ready to launch. The mentor offers the mentee a safe place to identify and plant her own Hope-Markers. As mentors, we are invited in by God to travel alongside the mentee on a portion of her journey. With feet firmly planted on the mentoring path with love, wisdom, and the call of God for the relationship, a mentor can serve as a powerful guide towards healing, restoration, and hope in a mentee's life that will not only affect her present, but also the trajectory of her future.

We will then see our mentees newly encouraged,

empowered, and grounded in the Word of God. They will be ready to launch into life with a God-perspective that has been inspired by the planting of their own Hope-Markers. We will see our purpose in this relationship fulfilled, no matter where life leads. Mentor and mentee will be forever bonded, woven together into God's rich tapestry of His master plan for this world. Then both mentor and mentee wait on God's next assignment: a new mentee for each to encourage.

We all are called to love God above all else in our lives. By aligning the priorities of our life to this truth, we will find navigation of our way along God's path for our life will become much easier. Sharing this truth and the effect it has on our lives is the perfect love of 1 John 4:19.

Endorsements

"This inspiring book offers much encouragement to its readers. In a world that seems hopeless, Joan has demonstrated ways to discover hope in the people and events which surround us. They are our "hope markers" and they can be found in our trials as well as our triumphs. She has a heart for God and a call to mentor women, urging them to share their stories with others. Whether you are a speaker, writer or you share your testimony one-on-one, Joan's book will stir the fire within you to serve Jesus Christ. "Hope Markers" will not only give you hope, but it will boost your desire to spread hope in your part of the world."

Carolyn Dale Newell
Christian author/speaker
www.amountainoffaith.wordpress.com

"Using personal stories, Joan Gallagher writes a heartfelt message, encouraging women to affirm the people and events in their lives God uses to bring them hope. Reminding us to be hope givers as well as receivers, she affirms both those who can mentor and also those who long for a mentor to take them under the wing. Readers will be engaged in the stories and soon find themselves reflecting on the Hope-Markers in their own lives."

Tricia Scribner: MA Apologetics, MS Nursing, Author of
Woman to Woman: Preparing Yourself to Mentor

"Gallagher has done a phenomenal job at helping us to see the markers of hope that can carry us from hope to hope and grace to grace along our life journeys. She has given a truly inspiring dialogue in literary form for those of us who are sparse in our recalling of the hope that carries us through the God who loves us."

J.E. Berry, Speaker and Author of
The Truth About Happiness

"Joan shows how our life stories, once repurposed under the Spirit's renewal, can honor God, create hope, and mentor others. Mentors will find this an inspirational and helpful guide for meaningful conversations with next generation women."

Dr. Barbara Neumann serves as a professor in the Educational Ministries and Leadership department at Dallas Theological Seminary

"With the tenacity of a competitive athlete, Joan Gallagher pursues the drifting soul. Through sharing her own story, and encouraging others to do the same, she offers encouragement, healing and inspiration. She fights fiercely to point others to the ultimate source of hope. I can tell you from personal experience, her enthusiasm is contagious and her passion for mentoring is genuine. Joan challenges others to embrace their own story and allow God use their pasts in order to shape their futures. Her story is important and her book will show you how yours is too."

Vickie Petz Henderson, M.D. Speaker, Author of "Dressing the Wound: Give Yourself the Gift of Forgiveness," Host of "My Journey of Faith Radio"

Website: www.vickiepetzhenderson.com
Blogs at www.myupsiderightlife.com

Made in the USA
Charleston, SC
18 February 2017